CONTENTS

First published 1981
Reprinted 1982, 1984
© John Addison 1981
ISBN 0 7134 2485 0

Printed and bound in Great Britain
by Anchor Brendon Ltd, Tiptree, Essex
for the publishers B.T. Batsford Limited
4 Fitzhardinge Street, London W1H 0AH

ACKNOWLEDGMENTS

The Author and Publishers thank the following for their kind permission to use the illustrations in this book: Africana Museum, Johannesburg, for the photograph on page 13 (right); Associated Press Ltd, page 59; BBC Hulton Picture Library, page 18; D. Le Breton, page 21; Camera Press Ltd, pages 17, 27, 31, 33, 37 (top), 45, 48 (top right), 54 (bottom), 55 (top), 56 (bottom), 60; Cape Times Ltd, page 29; R.D. Crooks, page 44; International Defence and Aid Fund, pages 4, 24, 36, 41, 47, 48 (left), 50 (top), 52, 53, 54 (top), 55 (bottom); Keystone Press Agency Ltd, pages 14, 20, 42, 49, 50 (bottom), 56 (top); Mansell Collection Ltd, pages 11, 22, 23; Popperfoto, pages 5, 15, 34, 48 (bottom), 63; The South African Library, Cape Town, page 13 (left). The maps were drawn by Chartwell Illustrators.

INTRODUCTION

In writing about South Africa it is important to use the words describing different groups of people accurately and consistently. For these words can often reflect and betray a writer's attitudes and, perhaps, prejudices.

Throughout this book the word "Africans" is normally used to describe the black peoples of South Africa. It is the word which the black inhabitants themselves prefer. It has the advantage of being free of the derogatory tone of most of the alternatives.

Other terms are explained in the Glossary on page 68.

"Apartheid" is an Afrikaans word. Afrikaans is the language which was evolved by the descendants of the original Dutch settlers in South Africa. In 1925 it replaced Dutch as one of the country's two official languages. The other is English. The word "apartheid" was invented in the early 1940s when it was used occasionally by Afrikaans newspapers and National Party politicians to describe the kind of racial policy they favoured. It was adopted by the National Party to describe its racial policies in the period immediately before the election of 1948. The National Party was dominated by Afrikaner Nationalists and was the political arm of Afrikaner Nationalism. The surprise victory of the party in 1948 and the adoption of apartheid were closely linked. Together these developments made 1948 a significant year in South Africa's history.

"Apartheid" means literally "apartness" or "separateness". It basically describes the system which, theoretically, aims to separate the white and non-white peoples of South Africa and divides the country into separate areas for occupation and ownership by whites — "white" South Africa; Africans — the "Bantustans" or Bantu "homelands"; and Coloureds and Asians. The system also controls, in the interests of the white minority, the economic life of the country, particularly the supply of African labour to white industry.

But neither this nor any other attempt to define "apartheid" will be generally acceptable. Different people will see and explain and interpret it differently, depending on their class, colour, nationality and so on. One thing is certain: it quickly aroused strong feelings both inside and outside South Africa and among people of different races. By 1960 it had become one of the "dirtiest" words in the world, to such an extent that the South African Prime Minister, Dr Verwoerd, tried to drop it. A few short definitions or descriptions by supporters and opponents of apartheid will show how controversial the policy became. First, here is an official definition put out in 1948 by the National Party:

> The policy of apartheid is a concept historically derived from the experience of the established White population of the country, and in harmony with such Christian principles as justice and equity. It is a policy which sets itself the task of preserving and safeguarding the racial identity of the White population of the country; of likewise preserving and safeguarding the identity of the indigenous peoples as separate racial groups, with opportunities to develop into self-governing national units; of fostering the inculcation of national consciousness.

This is a South African historian's summary of the Nationalists' justification for apartheid:

> The theory of apartheid is that white and non-white are so dissimilar in culture that they

3

can never live together as a community. If they were to try, the numerically strong non-whites would swamp the whites politically, culturally and economically. The only solution, therefore, is to partition the country into areas where whites alone will have full rights and privileges. (Leo Marquand *The Story of South Africa,* Faber, London, 1970, p. 242.)

A very critical view was expressed by one of the white MPs representing Africans in Parliament:

The policy appears to me as simply and obviously a cheap labour policy. As such, in its long term range, it is essentially oppression and I do not see how anybody can defend it as anything else. (Mrs Margaret Ballinger in the House of Assembly, Cape Town, 1948.)

Another white historian saw apartheid as "a cloak" for the economic exploitation of Africans:

The reality of the situation under apartheid is white domination with the whites forming a racist oligarchy and the Bantustans [the name for the Bantu homelands] a source of labour for white industry . . . . Unless the South African Government can show more responsible returns for separate development one cannot but conclude that the whole endeavour is a monstrous hoax. (Professor Dunbar Moodie, *The Rise of Afrikanerdom,* University of California Press, 1975.)

A famous black leader, Nelson Mandela, condemned the Bantustans as instruments for the oppression of Africans:

The Bantustans are not intended to voice the aspirations of the African people; they are instruments for their subjection. Under the pretext of giving them self-government the African peoples are being split up into tribal units in order to retard their growth and

Nelson Mandela (left) dedicated his life to the fight for African rights. Here he is shown with another black African leader, Walter Sisulu, in prison on Robben Island a few miles off Cape Town.

development into full nationhood. (Nelson Mandela, *No Easy Walk to Freedom,* Heinemann, 1965.)

A United States diplomat at the United Nations in 1959 called apartheid a legalized violation of human rights:

> Apartheid is a violation of human rights, buttressed and sanctified by law.

Important as the changes in South Africa in 1948 were, they can be exaggerated. It can be argued that "apartheid" was little more than a new word to describe a policy whose roots go far back into South African history. Previously the policy had been known as "separation" or "segregation". Moreover, every South African government since the Union of South Africa in 1910 had been led by an Afrikaner with a largely Afrikaner cabinet. In 1948 Dr Malan's cabinet was made up exclusively of Afrikaners. Neither the launching of the policy of apartheid nor the victory of the National Party in the 1948 election constituted a drastic break with the past.

Events of 1948 also increased the danger that South African history would be distorted, in two respects. They focused attention on the government's aim of keeping the different racial groups apart. But it is essential to realize that, in practice, the effectiveness of this policy has always been limited. Indeed, as will be argued later, and as is suggested by some of the critical descriptions above, those who designed the policy never intended that it should separate whites and non-whites in an absolute sense. Rather, they were trying to ensure that the whites would be in a position to dominate and exploit the non-whites more effectively than before. In fact, since the arrival of the first white settlers in 1652, the ways in which whites and blacks in

5

South Africa have mingled and interacted have been of greater importance for the country's growth and development than any attempts to keep them artificially apart. The truth of this can be illustrated by two very basic facts about South Africa. First, there are about 2½ million Coloured people in the country today. These are the product of inter-breeding of the white and non-white peoples of South Africa over a period of more than three hundred years. Second, South Africa is by far the richest and most highly industrialized country in Africa. Its wealth and its industrial strength are the result of the economic integration and co-operation of the different races in the country. We shall see how one of the main aims of apartheid is to ensure that there is a ready supply of non-white labour to serve the needs of white-controlled industry.

A second distortion of history lies in the idea that apartheid is essentially and almost exclusively the result of Afrikaner attitudes and thinking, and that English-speaking whites disapprove of such policies and were not responsible for their development. In the sense that the Dutch were in South Africa for one hundred and fifty years before the British and that they had already begun to practise discrimination before the British took over the Cape in 1806, there is some justification for such an idea. For thirty years after 1806 certain aspects of British policy created the impression that the British treated the Africans more humanely than the "Boers" did. Thereafter, however, and particularly after the discovery of diamonds and gold had attracted more British immigrants, there was little justification for such views. Yet the fact that apartheid, South Africa's racial policy in its most recent and highly developed form, was particularly associated with the Afrikaner-dominated National Party has allowed the old myth to persist.

This introduction should have made one point clear: it does not make sense to begin a study of apartheid in 1948. Apartheid is no more than the latest version of policies that have evolved over a long period of time. It is impossible to understand these policies without some knowledge of South Africa's early history. It is time, therefore, to turn back to the main developments in that history and, in particular, to try to trace the interaction of the different racial groups that have played a part in the story.

THE PEOPLES OF SOUTH AFRICA

Today four main racial groups live within the boundaries of the Republic of South Africa. These are the Africans (or the "Bantu" or blacks); the Europeans (divided mainly into those of Dutch descent — the Boers or Afrikaners, and those of British descent); the Coloureds (descendants of mixed unions between whites and non-whites, sometimes called Cape Coloureds because the Cape is where most of them were born and still live today); and Asians (mainly Indians). Many white South Africans would object to describing the black people as "Africans". They themselves, they would argue, are just as entitled to this description. Moreover, the blacks are not one ethnic group or nation, but several: Zulu, Xhosa, Venda, Swazi, Sotho, Tswana, and others.

The four main groups above are listed according to their numerical strength. In 1977 there were about 20 million Africans, just over 4 million Europeans, 2½ million Coloureds and about ¾ million Asians. Another basic fact about the four groups is the date of their arrival within the present boundaries of South Africa. Though disputes about political and other rights can rarely be settled by arguments based on earliest occupation, such an argument is certainly put forward by whites in South Africa to justify the whole system of apartheid and the privileged position it gives them. In particular, it is used to explain the unequal distribution of land between blacks and whites. It is now beyond dispute that these claims of whites are very weak ones.

Archaeological and other evidence has shown that the expanding Bantu-speaking peoples migrating from further north in search of more land crossed the river Limpopo, the present northern boundary of South Africa, round about the fourth century AD. By the fifth century, Early Iron Age Bantu-speakers were living in many parts of the northeastern Transvaal and the north of Natal. Later Iron Age sites have been found from about 1000 AD onwards in parts of the Highveld and on the hills and ridges of Natal. In the fifteenth century what is now the very heart of "white" South Africa, the southern Transvaal, was quite thickly populated by Bantu-speaking Africans who were building stone dwellings. When Portuguese sailors first rounded the Cape and sailed up the coast of Natal at the end of the fifteenth century, they found the same Africans as far south as the site of modern Port Elizabeth.

The first white settlers landed at the Cape in 1652. They did not reach the Gamtoos and Fish rivers in the eastern Cape until the eighteenth century. The Coloured people date from soon after the arrival of the whites. The first Asians were Malays and others from South East Asia. They came as superior slaves, from the late seventeenth century. The largest group of Asians came as indentured or contract labourers from India, to work on the sugar plantations in Natal. They began to arrive in 1860 and continued to come until 1911.

The earliest inhabitants of what is now South Africa did not belong to any of the four groups mentioned above. They were the more primitive African peoples who were still either hunter-gatherers or pastoralists when the first white settlers arrived and began to encounter them near the Cape. The Dutch contemptuously called them "Bushmen" and "Hottentots". Today these names are regarded as derogatory and "San" (Bushmen) and "Khoikhoi" — or "Khoi" — (Hottentots) are used instead. These words are taken from the language of the Khoikhoi. The term "Khoisan" is sometimes used collectively for the two peoples. Many of the San were slaughtered in conflicts with the Dutch, and those who remained retreated into the inhospitable desert and semi-desert lands of what are now Namibia and Botswana.

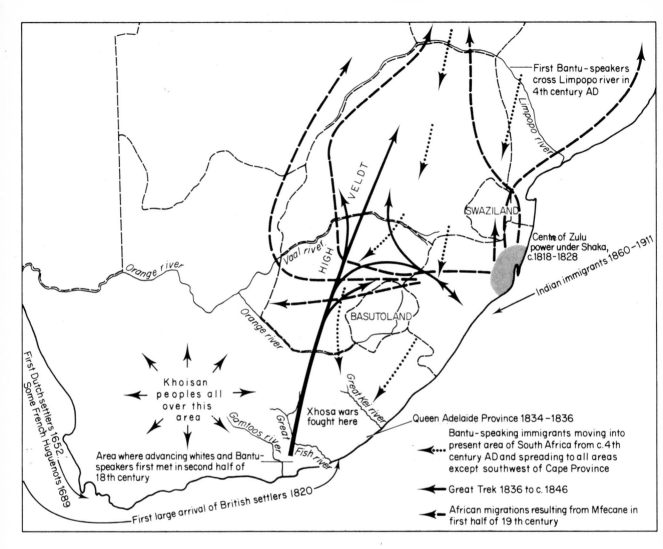

Map labels:
- First Bantu-speakers cross Limpopo river in 4th century AD
- Limpopo river
- VELDT
- HIGH
- SWAZILAND
- Centre of Zulu power under Shaka, c.1818-1828
- Indian immigrants 1860-1911
- Vaal river
- Orange river
- Orange river
- BASUTOLAND
- Great Kei river
- Khoisan peoples all over this area
- Xhosa wars fought here
- Gamtoos river
- Great Fish river
- Queen Adelaide Province 1834-1836
- First Dutch settlers 1652. Some French Huguenots 1689
- Area where advancing whites and Bantu-speakers first met in second half of 18th century
- First large arrival of British settlers 1820

Legend:
- •••• Bantu-speaking immigrants moving into present area of South Africa from c.4th century AD and spreading to all areas except southwest of Cape Province
- ◄— Great Trek 1836 to c.1846
- ◄-- African migrations resulting from Mfecane in first half of 19th century

Movement of peoples into and within South Africa in the last two thousand years.

Most of the Khoikhoi were eventually absorbed by other more advanced peoples. Thus, except immediately around modern Cape Town and the Cape Peninsula, the idea that the whites have any claim to dominance on grounds of earlier occupation is a myth. Elsewhere the Africans, whether San, Khoikhoi or Bantu-speakers, were there first.

The Dutch at the Cape

The Dutch East India Company established its small colony at the Cape in 1652, as a refreshment station for its ships calling there on the long voyage to and from the East Indies. The Company expected its settlers to grow vegetables and to obtain meat by barter from the Africans. Contacts with the Africans, however, were to be limited and friendly. Trading companies existed to make profits. Trouble with native peoples could easily lead to heavy expense and fighting. The first settlement of Dutch colonists at the Cape is a good example of a limited project which had quite unforeseen consequences.

Within five years the Company's original settlers were failing to provide the fresh food supplies needed by the Company's ships calling at the Cape. Jan van Riebeek, the Governor, made two changes in 1657. He imported slaves from West Africa to do the work which the Company's servants were too lazy to perform. This began to establish a traditional relationship between whites and blacks. White men were masters: black men were slaves or servants and performed unskilled work. Van Riebeek also allowed a small group of the Company's servants to become "free burghers". They were given a limited amount of land and expected to supply the Company's needs. Restrictions were placed on their freedom. They were not allowed to trade direct with the Khoi. Only the Company could do this. Van Riebeek planted a hedge of bitter almond trees around the small settlement to keep out the Khoi. It was the first of many attempts to keep the races apart.

The Boers spread

In these early days, however, as in more recent times, economic needs and pressures were more powerful than legal restrictions or physical barriers and boundaries. By the end of the seventeenth century the number of burghers had increased to about six hundred. Some two hundred Huguenots had arrived in 1688, refugees from religious persecution in France. They brought new skills to the community, notably that of cultivating the vine and making wine. Culturally they were soon absorbed by the more numerous Dutch settlers. By the early eighteenth century the Company's control over the burghers was breaking down. Their economic prospects were bleak. The market for produce at the Cape was very limited and monopolized by the Company. In spite of restrictions, the burghers traded with the Khoi to obtain cattle. These they used as a means to self-sufficiency. They turned their backs on the Cape and began to trek in search of grazing land for their cattle. The era of the "trekboer" had begun. With guns to protect themselves against the Khoi or the San; with their cattle to provide food and other basic needs; with their covered wagons and teams of oxen to carry their families and their possessions, they moved eastwards or northwards among the Khoi and the San. With their superior weapons they took land from the Khoi. Some were killed. Others, having lost their land, had no alternative but to work for the Boers on their vast ranches. Six thousand acres came to be recognized as a Boer's birthright. The practice of reducing the amount of land available to Africans became a recognized means of forcing them to offer their labour to whites (page 22).

Boer families tended to be large. The population grew. Sons trekked to carve out farms for themselves on the same lavish scale as their father's. The trekking process continued, with little official check, until a variety of obstacles were encountered. Northeast of the Cape it was not long before the Boers came up against land so dry and barren that it could not satisfy their needs. More important, however, in the second half of the eighteenth century the trekkers began to encounter in increasing numbers a different kind of African, the Bantu-speakers. The name "Bantu" comes from the language spoken by Africa's most numerous group of negroes. Common to all of them is the word "ntu": a person. The prefix "ba" makes a word plural. "Bantu" therefore means "men" or "people". Among the southeastern Bantu-speakers there were three main sub-divisions. These were the Nguni, who had kept to the coastal lowlands between the Drakensberg escarpment and the Indian Ocean; the Sotho, who moved across the Veld or grassland west of the escarpment; and the Tswana, further west still, some, though not all, on poorer land which eventually merged into the great southwestern desert.

The Bantu-speakers were more advanced than either the San or the Khoi. They were farmers, growing some crops but mainly keeping animals. They worked metals, especially iron, and made pottery. They lived in larger communities and were organized, under chiefs, in clans and tribes. Above all, however, they were much more numerous and offered a serious obstacle to the trekking habits of the Boers. The first group facing the Boers across the Fish river were the Xhosa. Like the Boers, they kept cattle, and they wanted more land.

The Dutch authorities at the Cape had feared this sort of confrontation for a long time without being able to do much about avoiding it. From time to time they had tried to halt the advance of the farmers. In 1778, for example, Governor Plettenberg tried to make the Great Fish river a frontier. It was already too late. For many years there had been movement across it in both directions by Boers, Xhosa and Khoikhoi, and the races were mingled in the area between the

Gamtoos and Great Fish rivers. There had been contact between the different peoples, some of it peaceful, some violent. There was trading and social mixing, including the occasional marriage. In the long run conflict was always likely because of rivalry and competition for land and trade. In 1779 the first of a series of wars was fought. These were the Xhosa wars, often referred to as the "Kaffir" wars by white South Africans. ("Kaffir" is an Arabic word for "black" and its use is particularly resented by Africans.) The wars spanned a period of nearly one hundred years.

The immediate cause of the earlier ones was usually cattle raiding and counter-raiding, but land and trade were other issues. The Dutch had already clashed with the San and the Khoikhoi. These conflicts had been resolved by the slaughter or expulsion of the former and the capture or assimilation of the latter. Many of the Khoikhoi became servants of the Dutch and their separate cultural identity began to disappear fairly quickly. Neither of these solutions was possible in the case of the much more numerous Bantu-speakers.

THE GREAT TREK

By 1793 two Xhosa wars had been fought. A far greater war had broken out in Europe between the French, under their new revolutionary government, and much of Europe. In 1794 the French overran Holland. The British, determined that the French should not also seize Holland's overseas possessions, occupied the Cape. It was temporarily returned in 1803 but re-occupied in 1806 and retained by Britain when peace was made in 1815. By 1836 relations between the trekboers and the British authorities had become so strained that some fourteen thousand Boers moved northwards out of the old colony. This movement was called the Great Trek. It was much more than a revival, on a larger scale, of the old Boer habit of trekking. The main thing which drove most of the fourteen thousand Boers northwards across the Orange river and the vaguely recognized boundary of the Cape Province was a desire to free themselves from the intolerable interference of the British in their way of life. Piet Retief, the greatest of the Boer leaders, wrote in his Manifesto explaining their action: "We quit this colony under the full assurance that the English Government has nothing more to require of us, and will allow us to govern ourselves without its interference in future". It was wishful thinking. The Great Trek marked the beginning rather than the end of a long and bitter rivalry between the two white peoples of South Africa. It overshadowed the racial rivalry between black and white for the remainder of the nineteenth century.

British-Boer relations at the Cape

It was not surprising that friction developed

The Great Trek. In four years between 1836 and 1840 nearly fourteen thousand Boers trekked northwards out of the Cape Colony in search of new homes. A nation was on the move.

between the two white groups. For a century or more before the British arrived, the Boer farmers lived in increasing isolation. They were cut off from the changing world of western Europe, the world of the early days of the industrial and agricultural revolutions; of the "Enlightenment" and the French Revolution. Boer minds grew narrow and closed as European minds were liberated and opened up. The Bible was the only reading matter of the Boers and the Old Testament had a deep influence on their thinking and on their characters. In their struggle with the forces of nature, with the local peoples, and, occasionally, with the authorities at the Cape, they came to see themselves — like the children of Israel — as a chosen people in search of a promised land and the fulfilment of a glorious destiny. In their isolation they began to evolve a language of their own, Afrikaans. By the end of the nineteenth century, when Afrikaners, as the Boers were called by that time, were beginning to acquire a sense of nationhood, their historians looked back on these early days and incorporated episodes from them into their "Sacred History of the Afrikaner Nation".

When the British returned as rulers of the Cape in 1806, the missionary era in southern Africa had already begun. The missionaries made their own contribution to the growth of Anglo-Boer hostility. In particular, they outraged the Boers by interfering in the traditional relationship between masters and servants, whites and blacks. They accused Boer farmers of ill-treating their slaves and Khoikhoi servants, and at the court hearings during the "Black Circuit" of 1813 charges were brought by slaves and servants against their masters, with the backing and encouragement of missionaries. Two years later, in 1815, a minor rebellion grew out of the refusal of a farmer to answer a summons. The episode ended with the execution of five Boers at Schlacter's Nek. Later this story was to have a prominent place in the "Sacred History".

The best-known of the missionaries was Dr John Philip who took up his post as head of the London Missionary Society mission in 1819. He was a typical evangelical Christian of the time. He believed in the equality of all men and strongly disapproved of slavery. He has been credited with too much influence in the passing of the Fiftieth Ordinance in 1828, a law which became known as the "Hottentots' Charter". It gave them equality before the law, removed the requirement that they should carry passes and set them free to sell their labour where they chose. It was passed at a time when there was a shortage of labour on white farms. Boer resentment knew no bounds, and the measure was more important in South Africa than the Act for the Emancipation of Slavery six years later, which came as an anti-climax. Philip was an advocate of segregation at a time when, given the establishment of an effective frontier, it might still have achieved what he wanted. He saw segregation as the best hope of preventing further exploitation of the Africans in South Africa. In 1834 Governor Durban's decision to annex Queen Adelaide Territory was opposed by Philip and welcomed by the Boers. The enforced return of the land, under orders from the Colonial Secretary, was welcomed by Philip. It was the last straw so far as the Boers were concerned. The Great Trek was on.

The Great Trek
The Great Trek put an end to any hope of segregation as Dr Philip envisaged it. The racial map of South Africa was transformed and the pattern of settlement became much more complex than it had been before. White men occupied large areas of the high and low veld between the Orange and Limpopo rivers and of the lower land in Natal. Much of the land they settled appeared to be unoccupied and unused. This was deceptive, however. It was often a temporary phenomenon caused by the flight of Bantu-speaking peoples from the attacks of Shaka's fierce Zulu impis during the Mfecane or "Time of Crushing". This helped the whites to establish the myth that they were the first occupants of these lands. As conditions became more stable after Shaka's death, some of the displaced inhabitants returned, particularly to parts of Natal. The Mfecane had at least as important an effect on the redistribution of peoples in South Africa as the Great Trek.

If at times the trekkers took possession of land that was, for the moment, unoccupied, they also seized land by right of conquest, after clashing

Shaka (left) and Moshesh (right): two great black African leaders in the early nineteenth century. Shaka, the "Black Napoleon", able but cruel, terrorized neighbouring peoples in the 1820s and moulded the Zulus and many of their captives into a formidable military state. Moshesh had a talent for diplomacy and an eye for the defensive value of his mountainous country. His skill enabled his people to survive as a nation. He sought, and obtained, British protection: the right to become "a flea in the Great Queen's blanket".

with groups of Bantu-speakers. Potgieter's party defeated Mzilikazi's Ndebele in the Transvaal and sent them on their way to their final home in what later became part of Rhodesia. A prolonged rivalry developed between the Boers and Moshesh, the great leader of the Sotho. Under his skilful leadership, the Sotho survived as a nation in the mountains of their homeland and eventually obtained some security under British protection. This was only after much fighting and the loss of some of their land to the Boers.

The Great Trek as a whole has a central place in the epic history of the Afrikaner nation. The most famous episode of all was Pretorius's victory at the Battle of Blood River on 16 December 1838. It was a battle fought to avenge the treacherous attack by Dingaan's Zulus on Piet Retief's party earlier in the year. Before the battle the trekkers promised that, if victorious, they would celebrate with an annual service of thanksgiving. In 1952 Dingaan's Day was belatedly renamed the "Day of the Covenant".

The British at the Cape

For nearly twenty years after the start of the Great Trek the British reaction to it was uncertain. Conflicting considerations tugged in different directions. Powerful among them was the fear that, if the Boers were left free to practise their own harsh racial policies, serious conflict between blacks and whites would follow and these could be disastrous for the whites. Finally, in 1852 and 1854, fear of the growing involvement in such conflicts and in further expansion

Basutoland. A typical landscape in the homeland of the Sotho (Basuto) people. Their mountainous country helped them to resist the trekboers.

led the British to recognize the independence of two Boer states: the Orange Free State and the Transvaal. At last it seemed that the trekkers had achieved the main purpose of the Great Trek and shaken off the hated British yoke.

In the meantime the British had annexed Natal and, after little more than eight years in this "Promised Land", the Boers who had settled there trekked once again back over the Drakensberg escarpment and into the Transvaal. After 1845 Shepstone, Diplomatic Agent to the Tribes of Natal, spent over thirty years shaping the colony's racial policy. He put into operation the first segregation policy attempted on a large scale. Many Africans returned to Natal in the 1840s after a temporary absence following Shaka's wars. By 1860 about eighty thousand of them were settled in areas which were called "Native Reserves". These had an area of about

2¾ million acres. Another sixty thousand Africans lived on Crown lands (lands seized by the British government, technically, because they seemed to be unoccupied) or settled as squatters on white farms. The total area of Natal was about 12½ million acres. When Natal was given a legislative council in 1856, the franchise was theoretically open to Africans; but the qualifications were so numerous and the procedure so daunting that no more than a handful of Africans ever obtained the right to vote. Shepstone claimed that his policy protected Africans from exploitation and preserved their traditional way of life, but race discrimination was as blatantly practised by the British in Natal as by the Boers in their two republics. Only in the Cape Province, where representative government was introduced in 1854, was the franchise granted to members of all races on the same terms. It was a "civilized" vote, depending partly on wealth and partly on education. The Cape's comparative liberalism already stood out clearly in contrast to the position in the other three territories.

DIAMONDS AND GOLD; THE BOER WARS; THE UNION OF SOUTH AFRICA

Industrialization

The Great Trek and the Mfecane together had revolutionized the pattern of settlement in South Africa, but they had not yet created the present-day pattern. One great formative influence had still to do its work. In 1860 South Africa remained an overwhelmingly rural and agricultural society. Much of the farming was for subsistence; but wool, skins, hides and ivory were exported. There was little industry or manufacturing and most of it was for the processing of agricultural products like the milling of flour and the washing of wool; or to meet local needs by making wagons or furniture or by quarrying

Market day, Kimberley, 1888. Kimberley grew up rapidly after the discovery of diamonds in 1867. The discovery of minerals changed the character of South Africa's society and its economic life.

stone. Today South Africa is the most industrialized country in Africa. The transition began in the last thirty years of the nineteenth century, with the discovery of rich mineral deposits, particularly diamonds and gold.

Diamonds were found in 1867 near the confluence of the Orange and Vaal rivers, in an area where the land was so poor that its ownership was uncertain. Gold was found on the Witwatersrand in the Transvaal in 1886. These two discoveries quickly transformed the economic and social life of South Africa and the balance of power between the four territories. There was a rush of prospectors from other parts of South Africa and from abroad. Africans came into the area in even larger numbers than whites, to provide the labour for digging. The white population of South Africa doubled between 1871 and 1891. Two bustling new industrial towns, Kimberley and Johannesburg sprang up. Railways were built to link the ports to the mining areas. By 1894 Johannesburg was connected by rail to Cape Town, Durban, East London and Port Elizabeth in the British territories and, to diminish the Boers' dependence on Britain, to Lourenco Marques in Portuguese Mozambique. The new urban population created a new market for food and started a boom in agriculture. African peasants as well as white farmers benefitted briefly from the new situation.

Labour for the mines

A prosperous African peasantry was, however, a threat to the white economy and its needs. Apart from competing with white farmers, prosperous African peasants would no longer have any desire to work on white farms or in the new mines. The mining industry had begun to require large quantities of African labour, because of the unique character of the South African gold mines. Gold exists in greater quantities there than anywhere else in the world; but it is difficult and costly to extract. It is found at a great depth and in combination with vast quantities of rock. The great spoil heaps around Johannesburg and elsewhere testify to this. A plentiful supply of cheap labour has always been necessary for the economic working of the mines. From the start Africans have supplied the labour and the gold mining industry could not have prospered without them.

From an early date the mining companies discovered that the cheapest and, therefore, from their point of view, the best kind of labour, was migrant labour. This system was organized and perfected by the Chamber of Mines, who hired labourers on short contracts, not only from the African reserves in the four territories of South Africa but also from the British protectorates of Basutoland, Swaziland and Bechuanaland and from further afield in Mozambique and Nyasaland (now Malawi). The system worked so well that it is used still today. From the African's point of view, it is an inhuman system. Workers leave their homes and families for periods of perhaps several months to live in compounds with other male workers. In the towns they have no rights. Families are split, and African societies and traditional life suffer. So, the urban black worker and temporary urban resident, without rights, had made his appearance on the South African scene. The pattern of settlement and of the social and economic scene was being completed.

The Boer Wars

The discovery of diamonds and gold also had a powerful impact on relations between the Boers and British. They had improved for a short period, following Britain's recognition of the two Boer Republics in the 1850s, but relations now deteriorated again leading eventually to two wars. In 1871, after some dispute about ownership of Griqualand where the diamonds had been discovered, the British annexed it and later handed it over to the Cape Colony which was granted self-government in 1872. The Boers in the Orange Free State and the Transvaal, who had also claimed the territory, were bitter about the annexation. It was seen as a typical example of British imperial greed and aggression. Anglo-Boer relations, already strained by the British declaration of a protectorate over Basutoland in 1868, worsened. The new problems and responsibilities brought by the rush of both blacks and whites to the diamond area revived Britain's plans for a federation of South African states.

This now became Britain's policy in South Africa. The need for whites to adopt a common policy towards Africans seemed urgent. There was a growing danger that the sparsely populated Transvaal might be overwhelmed by African neighbours. This gave Britain the pretext for re-annexing the Transvaal in 1877, when a new warlike mood seemed to be developing among the Zulus, under their leader Cetchwayo. The move was tactlessly handled by the British, however,

The spoil heaps around modern Johannesburg are evidence of how difficult it is to extract South Africa's gold from the underground rock.

from start to finish. After the Zulus had been defeated in 1879 at Ulundi, the British delayed the restoration of independence to the Transvaal. The Boers grew impatient and defeated the British at Majuba Hill in the First War of Freedom, or the First Boer War. Limited independence was then restored to the Transvaal, but the British retained control of foreign policy and had a say in racial policy. Relations remained bad and prospects of a federation receded.

The beginning of the gold rush to the Witwatersrand after 1886 removed what little chance remained of establishing a federation. The rapid build-up of a brash, go-getting, noisy community in Johannesburg came as a shock to the quiet, deeply religious, backward society of Boer farmers. But at least it favoured them in one way. Almost overnight it made the Transvaal, hitherto

the poorest of the four white states in South Africa, by far the richest. Britain's earlier hopes that the Boers' poverty might tempt them into a federation with the more prosperous Cape were now gone. Moreover, in any future federation or union there was the obvious danger that it might be dominated by the Boers rather than by the British.

The Boers in the Transvaal were soon outnumbered by the influx of foreigners or "uitlanders", as the Boers called them. Paul Kruger, President of the Transvaal since 1883, was the embodiment of the now growing spirit of Afrikanerdom. Deeply religious, anti-British, narrow-minded, but inspired by a strong conviction of his people's destiny, he was determined that the unwanted new inhabitants should not gain control of the republic. The frustrations of the "uitlanders", many of them British, mounted as Kruger imposed more restrictions on their activities and refused to give them any

17

From the *Westminster Gazette.*] [January 9, 1896.
"THE NAPOLEON OF AFRICA." IS IT HIS MOSCOW?

Kruger (left) and Rhodes (right): white rivals for the domination of South Africa. As a boy, Kruger took part in the Great Trek and its anti-British spirit affected his attitude and politics throughout his life. Rhodes was one of Britain's greatest Empire builders. His dreams for British control and expansion of South Africa led him into his disastrous involvement in the Jameson Raid. This cartoon appeared shortly after the raid.

political rights. John Cecil Rhodes, who had already made a fortune in diamonds and gold, and became Prime Minister of the Cape in 1890, was frustrated for different reasons. His British South Africa Company was already pioneering in Rhodesia to the north of the Transvaal. He had ambitious dreams of extending British influence from the Cape to Cairo and Kruger's refusal to allow the railway to pass northwards through the Transvaal stood in his way. Impatient, Rhodes became involved in an ill-fated plot to overthrow Kruger's government, which ended with the fiasco of the Jameson Raid in December 1895. The secret of the conspiracy was badly kept. Kruger was ready for the attack and easily defeated it. Rhodes's political career in South Africa was prematurely ended. British complicity

was suspected. The world was hostile to Britain and the German Kaiser sent a provocative telegram of congratulations to Kruger. A show-down between the British and the Boers would have been difficult to avoid after this. With negotiations in the hands of Kruger for the Boers, and Milner, the British High Commissioner at the Cape, for the British, the chances of avoiding war were slight. Milner believed that if a federation or union of South Africa was to be achieved under British leadership and control, Afrikanerdom would first have to be smashed by force.

The Boers began their Second War of Freedom in 1899. It lasted longer than either side expected. During the war there were divisions inside both camps. Transvaalers and Freestaters felt that the Cape Afrikaners had let down their cause. As the war dragged on, there were rifts between the "hands-uppers", who wanted to seek peace, and the "bitter-enders", who wanted to fight to the last. In Britain the Liberal opposition was critical of the war and blamed it on aggressive imperialism. The years immediately after the war seemed to show that it had, on balance, strengthened and united the Afrikaners. A British sense of guilt partly explained the lenient peace of Vereeniging signed in 1902. Generous compensation helped the Boers to repair the ravages of war on their farms. There was equal recognition of the Dutch and English languages. Most important of all, in the long run, was the clause in which the British promised an early grant of responsible government to the two Boer territories. This was coupled with a promise that no decision could be taken about a non-European franchise until after the granting of responsible government.

The Union of South Africa

This promise removed any hope that non-whites would be given the vote in these territories. The truth was — and the next few years were to confirm this — that concern for African rights was not Britain's first priority. Her main aim after the war was to bring about a closer union of the white states of South Africa. She was aware of the strong opposition among the Afrikaners of the Transvaal and the Orange Free State to the grant of any political rights to non-Europeans. The British were anxious to begin the process of reconciliation. To some extent, Milner's policy of anglicizing South Africa threatened this process. His hope that returning prosperity would encourage large-scale British immigration was not realized. His attempt to establish English as the main language of education mis-fired. Afrikaners reacted strongly and set up the Christian National Education movement to defeat his schemes. Though limited funds restricted the number of its schools, the movement produced a generation of Afrikaners determined to preserve their culture and their national identity through their language and to fight British efforts to undermine them. Other signs of the rapid recovery of Afrikanerdom were seen in the emergence, in three of the four states, of powerful Afrikaner political parties. The oldest of these was the Afrikaner Bond in the Cape, soon to be broadened into the South Africa Party, to attract British support.

Botha and Smuts in the Transvaal founded *Het Volk* — the People, while Hertzog, another Boer War general, formed *Orangia Unie* in the Orange Free State. These last two parties, though launched by Afrikaners and finding their main support among them, were in favour of co-operation with the British.

The need for a new attempt to unite the four states seemed more pressing than ever. Customs barriers and transport restrictions did nobody any good and hampered economic recovery. Above all, the serious native rebellion that erupted in Natal in 1906, the Bambata Rebellion, underlined once again the need for an agreed racial policy. In 1908 a Constitutional Convention, with delegates from each of the main states, met at Durban to discuss the terms of a constitution for the Union of South Africa. The two Boer colonies had been granted self government in 1906-7, a magnanimous step by the new Liberal government in Britain, that won the gratitude of many Afrikaners. At the Convention the most controversial issue and the only one that threatened the success of the negotiations was that of the franchise. The delegates from the Cape, where a non-racial franchise had operated for over half a century, wanted their system to be extended to the other three states. The Transvaal and Orange Free State delegates would not hear of any political rights for non-Europeans; and the Natal delegation, though the most British of the four, sided with them. In the end, a one-sided compromise was reached. The Cape retained its "liberal" franchise, except that non-whites would not be eligible to stand for election. Elsewhere the franchise was for whites only. The Cape franchise was protected by an "entrenched" clause. It could only be changed by a two-thirds majority vote in a joint session of the two houses of the South African Parliament.

A few white voices were raised against the exclusion of non-whites from the mainstream of the political life of the Union. J.W. Sauer believed that, in the long run, the denial of justice to the Africans endangered the position of the whites: "Justice for the native would secure the position of the White man in South Africa for all time." Another famous Afrikaner, Jan Hendrik Hofmeyr, founder of the Afrikaner Bond Party in Cape

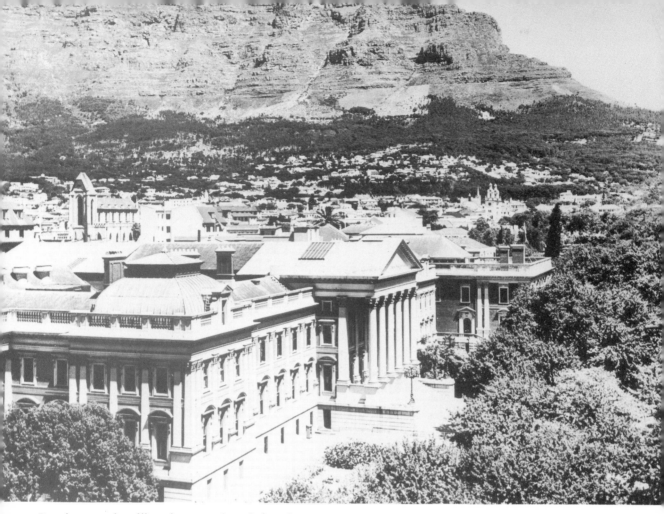

Parliament Buildings, Cape Town (left) and Government Buildings, Pretoria (right). To settle rival claims, the Union of South Africa was given three capitals: the legislative capital was at Cape Town; the administrative capital at Pretoria; and the judicial capital at Bloemfontein. The Parliament Buildings (left) overlook the site of the vegetable garden of the earliest Dutch settlers.

Province and a liberal, campaigned for the non-white franchise. Like Sauer, he believed that to deny the right to vote to the non-white peoples of South Africa was short-sighted. He wrote in 1909:

With a European population of only a million at the southern extremity of a continent occupied by some two hundred million, mostly barbarians and semi-barbarians, I cannot help feeling, whatever my own prejudices of race and colour may be, that the political and social security of South Africa would be none the worse for retaining the goodwill of the five million of Coloured and aboriginal inhabitants with whom we live interspersed, and for reconciling them with our political institutions. When the political union of all South Africa shall have been fully established, it would be a bad day for our new Commonwealth if in addition to protecting our northern frontiers against the teeming millions of Darkest Africa,

we had to be continually on our guard against a malcontent Coloured and Native population in our midst, outnumbering us by five or six to one. (Edgar Brookes, *Apartheid*, Routledge and Kegan Paul, London, 1969, p.165)

Having been accepted by the legislatures in all four states, the South Africa Bill had to be passed by the British Parliament. The general view was that, in spite of some misgivings about the franchise arrangements, it would be wrong to attempt to change a measure already passed by the four South African parliaments. At Westminster also there seemed to be an optimistic

feeling that in time Afrikaner racial attitudes would soften and the Cape franchise spread to the rest of the Union. The British government made a stand on only one issue. It refused to allow the three protectorates — Basutoland, Bechuanaland and Swaziland — to be incorporated into the Union under a constitution which discriminated so obviously against the African peoples. It was generally accepted, however, that circumstances would change in a way which would permit their inclusion in the near future. Neither this expectation, nor that

about the Cape franchise, was realized. Moreover, the device of the entrenched clause was not an effective protection for the non-white voters in the Cape. Albert Luthuli, the great African leader of the 1950s, passed this retrospective judgement on the South Africa Act:

This was the big divide, the great Segregation Act which set the pattern for subsequent discrimination and unjust laws that have made them [the Africans] political and social outcasts in their fatherland.

RACIAL POLICY 1910~1948

The South Africa Act

At the end of the Boer War in 1903, Milner set up a South African Native Affairs Commission, most of whose members were British, to advise on racial policy. Its report began with the assumption that white domination, already well established, would remain the basis of government policy. This would entail discrimination against non-whites in the political field. There should be no question of non-whites ever being numerous enough on a common voters' roll to outvote whites. If non-whites were given the right to vote, they should be placed on a separate or communal roll. In 1910 the political system of the Union was settled in its essentials by the South Africa Act. In three of the four provinces the non-whites were given no political rights. In the Cape, however, they were given voting rights on a common roll. It was one of the few respects in which the recommendations of Milner's Commission were not followed. However, the

position was to be changed later (see pages 30 and 38).

The Natives Land Act

The Commission went on to recommend the territorial separation of the races. To this end, reserves should be set aside and clearly defined for African ownership and occupation. The Commissioners linked this recommendation with the need to ensure a steady supply of labour for white farms and white industry. These closely linked questions of land and labour called for urgent attention in the years immediately after Union. They were tackled in 1913 in the Natives Land Act, one of the most basic of all South Africa's segregation measures. The act allocated 7.3 per cent of the land of the Union to the four million Africans out of a total population of about six million. This land was reserved solely for the occupation and use of Africans. Africans were forbidden to purchase any land

outside the reserves, and the practice of squatting on white land was stopped. An African would be allowed in a white area only for the purpose of working there. The South African government recognized that the amount of land set aside for Africans was hardly adequate, let alone generous, and appointed the Beaumont Land Commission to look into this in 1915. The Commission recommended that another 8 million morgen (a morgen was about 2½ acres) should be added to the original 10½ million morgen. However, nothing was done before 1936.

Africans believed that the main purpose of the Natives Land Act was to force them, in increasing numbers, to work on white farms and in the mines. General Louis Botha, the Prime Minister, denied this, but in a petition of protest presented to the government in 1914, the Rev. John Dube, President of the South African Native National Congress (founded in 1912 and later the African National Congress) maintained the charge:

> We make no protest against the principle of separation so far as it can be fairly and practically carried out. But we do not see how it is possible for this law to effect any greater separation between the races than obtains now. It is evident that the aim of this law is to compel service by taking away the means of independence and self-improvement. This compulsory service at reduced wages and high rents will not be separation, but an intermingling of the most injurious character of both races. (T. Karis & G.M. Carter, *From Protest to Challenge Vol. I*, Hoover Institution Press, 1972, p. 85.)

John Dube had in this paragraph identified the real purpose behind the measure. Some of the most fundamental legislation, while claiming to create the physical framework for separating the races, was deliberately creating the conditions which compelled blacks to sell their labour to whites.

African and white workers

For a short time after the First World War the South African economy flourished. But at the end of 1921 the price of gold fell and the mining industry faced trouble. The mining companies threatened to employ blacks in semi-skilled jobs in place of whites, with the intention of cutting the wage bill. The white trade unions had assumed that the Mines and Works Act of 1911 had reserved all such jobs for whites. In January 1922 white workers on the Rand came out on strike. The situation became threatening. Workers began drilling and forming commandos. There was talk of setting up a provisional government and proclaiming a republic. Early in March General Smuts, who had been Prime Minister since Botha's death in 1919, proclaimed martial law, sent troops into Johannesburg and took command. After three days of fighting and mass

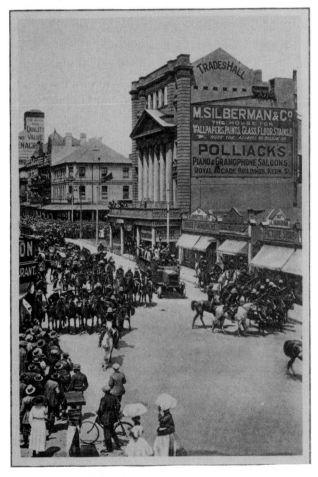

In the Rand Revolt in 1922 white workers on the Rand came out on strike to fight for their exclusive right to skilled and semi-skilled jobs. General Smuts, the Prime Minister, sent in troops to crush the strike: left: the scene after troops had bombarded and captured a strikers' stronghold at Fordsburg; right: the arrest of strike leaders at the Trades Hall in Johannesburg.

Living conditions for black mineworkers. Migrant black workers in the goldmines were housed in special compounds. Living accommodation was crowded and depressing, and, for security reasons, compounds were surrounded by wire fences.

arrests, order was restored and the strike broken.

The real victors were the companies. By reclassifying jobs and shuffling workers around, the mining magnates achieved their original purpose. In the 1924 general election, General Smuts was defeated by an alliance of Hertzog's Afrikaner Nationalists and the Labour Party. On coming to power, Hertzog and his "Pact" government had to pursue a policy which safeguarded the interests of white workers. It was called a "civilized labour" policy. A Mines and Works Amendment Act, passed in 1926 and usually known as the "Colour Bar" Act, prevented Africans and Asians from acquiring "certificates of competency" to perform responsible jobs in the mining industry.

Hertzog had come to power at a time when the problem of the "poor whites" was coming to a head. It had been building up slowly since the beginning of the century, but much more rapidly during the 1920s. The poor whites were mainly Afrikaners. For a variety of reasons they were forced off the land and came to seek work in the towns. They had no skills; and, without special consideration and protection, they were likely to remain unemployed. The answer to the problem lay partly in a civilized labour policy, but more in a big expansion of manufacturing industry, especially after the slump of the early 1930s was over. Whites became accustomed to the idea of doing unskilled manual work at "civilized" wages. Railways and municipalities were encouraged to offer jobs to poor whites which might previously have gone to blacks. In the long run, the rapid growth of manufacturing industries made such expedients less necessary. By the end of the 1930s the poor white problem had ceased to exist.

The reserves

There has always been the closest connection between the rapid growth of mining and manufacturing industries in South Africa and the existence of impoverished and inadequate African reserves. The reserves were reservoirs of cheap labour for white industry. Initially advocated by Dr Philip, and later by Shepstone, as a means of protecting the interests of the Africans, they had become a direct and effective means of exploiting them. Some features of traditional society may have survived on the reserves, but conditions forced thousands of Africans to seek work in white urban areas where their traditions were rapidly undermined.

In 1913 the Prime Minister, Botha, had refused to admit that the Natives Land Act was in any way intended to ensure a supply of labour for white farmers and white industrialists. Nevertheless, governments, industrialists and other employers have been well aware of the consequences of restricting the amount of land allocated to Africans. Through the Chamber of Mines, the gold-mining companies set up agencies for recruiting migrant workers systematically. Short-term contracts were signed by Africans and often renewed. Wages were very low and remained low over a long period. In 1943 underground African workers on the Rand were earning the same as they had done twenty years earlier — £2.95 a month. Since Africans were not allowed to strike, there was no way in which they could force their employers to pay them more. Also, it was argued that migrant workers' wages did not have to cover their families whose needs were provided for on the reserves. The reality was very different. Without the workers' earnings to bridge the gap, the families could hardly have survived.

The Africans also had to pay taxes. A poll tax was levied on every African male between the ages of eighteen and sixty-five, by the Native Taxation and Development Act, 1925. Taxation, which had to be paid in cash, was another device for forcing Africans to sell their labour to whites in return for a money wage. This was openly admitted in 1945 by the Social and Economic Planning Council: "One of the main objectives of Native taxation is, or was, to exert pressure on the Natives to seek work in agriculture, mining or manufacture. In this object it is probably very successful." The reserves had another economic and social role. Like a modern welfare state, they provided for the unemployed, the sick and the aged. When the migrant worker no longer served the needs of the whites he was simply sent "home" to the reserve. In 1922 the Stallard Commission on Local Government stated:

> The native should only be allowed to enter urban areas, which are essentially the White man's creation, when he is willing to enter and minister to the White man, and should depart therefrom when he ceases to minister.

The fact that the migrant worker left his wife and family on the reserve created a host of social problems. Husbands and wives, separated by the system, were subjected to strains and temptations that often wrecked family life. Unnatural burdens and responsibilities were placed on women both in the home and in the fields. Children without fathers were often ill-disciplined. Poverty bred crime. It also led to the spread of nutritional diseases.

In the white areas problems arose over housing the African workers. Mineworkers normally lived in compounds (see pictures opposite). The rest lived on the outskirts of industrial towns and cities in squalid, unhealthy shanty areas. It was not until 1923 that the government passed the first measure to tackle this problem. The Native Urban Areas Act placed responsibility for improving African housing on the local authorities. Improvement had to be carried out within the framework of a segregated location. The act made it clear that the workers were to be regarded as temporary residents. They could move in only under a system of "influx" control. They could be "endorsed out" when no longer required.

THE BIRTH OF APARTHEID

With the passing of the world economic crisis, an unprecedented economic boom began in South Africa and gathered momentum in the 1940s. The old-established mining industry recovered and expanded. More important still, a new sector of industry — secondary manufacturing industry — rapidly developed. It was accompanied by large-scale mechanization. In the decade 1940-50 the number of African workers on the Rand increased from six thousand to one million. This rapid expansion brought new problems as well as new wealth and new opportunities. It created new demands for skilled and semi-skilled labour. The arrival of large numbers of Africans in urban areas posed a potential threat to white domination and white control.

The end of segregation?
During the emergency period of the war African workers infiltrated many of the new jobs and the

Mining and industrial areas.

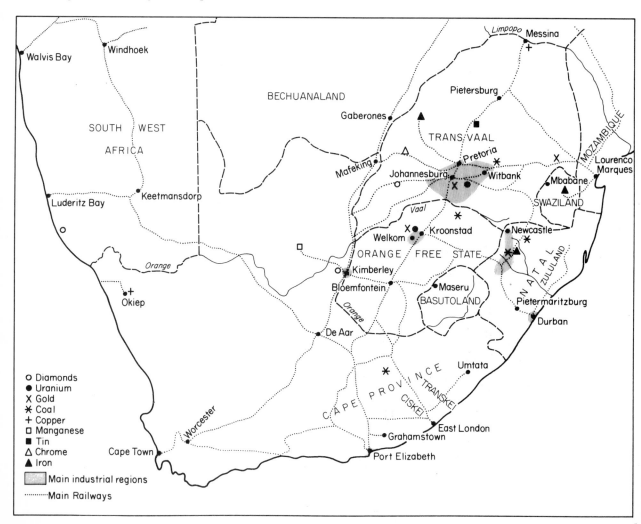

With the rapid expansion of industry in the late 1930s, large numbers of Africans came to work in the towns. They lived usually in improvised shacks, and shanty towns like this became a common sight on the outskirts of South Africa's cities and towns.

authorities turned a blind eye to what was happening. Industrialists began to argue that a colour bar in industry did not make economic sense, except to the white worker. They were critical of the system of migrant labour. How could industry find the stable and skilled work force it needed to maintain growth under such a system? Two important features of the system of segregation were under attack: the colour bar and migrant labour. In 1942 Smuts, once again Prime Minister and leader of the United Party, expressed the view that the more or less permanent urbanization of an increasing number of African workers was something that had to be accepted: "Segregation tried to stop it. It has, however, not stopped it in the least. The process has been accelerated. You might as well try to sweep the ocean back with a broom."

This was the kind of remark that played into the hands of those Nationalist politicians who had always argued that Smuts could not be trusted on racial policy and that he might put white supremacy at risk. Their suspicions were further roused when, in 1945, the Native Areas Consolidation Act defined the conditions under which an African could qualify for permanent residence in a town. These were: continuous residence since birth; continuous lawful residence for fifteen years; ten years' work with the same employer. Dependants of those who qualified in these ways were also eligible for permanent residence in the same area. To a really committed segregationist this was a dangerous concession.

Early in 1948, the year of the first post-war election, the Fagan or Native Laws Commission, appointed by Smuts in 1946, issued its report. Its conclusions were: that "the idea of total segregation is utterly impracticable"; that the migration from country to town is an economic necessity which cannot be stopped or reversed; that migrant labour is "a system which, in the long run, cannot be maintained otherwise than on a limited scale". The United Party accepted the conclusions of its own Commission. But, for the main Nationalist opposition under Dr Malan, this merely provided further timely evidence of what they had been warning white South Africans about for some time: Smuts and his party had become lax in enforcing segregation regulations. It was time to make a stand for the preservation of white standards and the maintenance of white supremacy.

The Sauer Report and "total segregation"

It was more than mere coincidence that the Sauer Report, commissioned by the National Party, appeared at almost the same time. In its introduction the report argued that there was only one choice for the country:

> The choice before us is one of these two divergent courses: either that of integration, which would in the long run amount to national suicide on the part of the Whites; or that of "apartheid", which professes to preserve the identity and safeguard the future of every race, with complete scope for everyone to develop within its own sphere while maintaining its distinctive national character.

The Sauer Report used the new word "apartheid" to refer to the policies it was advocating. It went out of its way to reassure the whites, rejecting the Fagan Report's view that "total segregation is utterly impracticable", and claiming: "The policy of our country should envisage total apartheid as the ultimate goal of a natural process of separate development". The National Party undertook to protect the whites "against any policy, philosophy or attack". It undertook to protect "the white character of our cities". The number of detribalized Africans would be frozen by strict influx control. The African in an urban area must be regarded as a visitor "who will never be entitled to any political rights or to equal social rights". A separate system of education was envisaged for Africans which would "take account of the needs and development of the mass of natives". African political representation would be limited to three nominated and four elected members of the Senate. Representation in the House of Assembly and the Native Representative Council would be abolished. To compensate for this loss of political representation in the South African Parliament, the Africans would be given a form of traditional government in the reserves. Urban Councils would be permitted with strictly limited powers. Notwithstanding any of this, the Sauer Report claimed that "this did not mean that the non-whites would be suppressed or exploited".

The 1948 election

Actually the two reports had much in common. Neither made any suggestion that voting rights should be restored to Africans. Both rejected any idea that the black workers should be allowed to strike. But the Sauer Report showed a greater confidence over the issue of migrant labour, and in the election of 1948 the white voter wanted to be reassured about the future of the whites in South Africa. The National Party raised the old scare of white supremacy being in danger. It created the impression that white civilization was unsafe in the keeping of Smuts and his vacillating policy. To their own surprise, as much as to that of their opponents, the Nationalists gained more seats in the election than any other party. With the support of the small Afrikaner Party, they had a clear majority. Smuts was stunned, but he had no doubts about the reason for his defeat. He put it down to "the poisonous fumes of apartheid".

THE RISE OF AFRIKANER NATIONALISM 1912~1948

Dr Malan was overjoyed at the election result. "Today", he said, "South Africa belongs to us once more. For the first time since Union South Africa is our own. May God grant that it will always remain so." Despite the fact that, since the Union in 1910, every Prime Minister had been an Afrikaner, those who regarded themselves as true Afrikaners had been unhappy about the extent of continuing British influence in their country. Botha and Smuts were regarded as traitors to the Afrikaner cause: they had betrayed the trust placed in them as leaders of the chosen people.

The Afrikaner Nationalist Party

General Hertzog felt this so strongly that, after serving for two years in Botha's cabinet, he left the government in 1912 to form the Afrikaner Nationalist Party. He quarrelled with the pro-British attitude of the government and wanted South Africa to pursue a much more independent course. In spite of this, he believed in a "two stream" policy. He wanted Afrikaners and British to work together while each preserving their own culture and identity. He was responsible for the replacement of Dutch by Afrikaans as the second official language in 1925.

At first, Hertzog's dislike of the British connection led him to advocate republicanism for South Africa. However, after he had returned from the Imperial Conference in London in 1926, his anti-British attitude softened. At the conference he had played a leading part in the adoption of the Balfour Declaration* as the basis of membership of the Empire. This declaration had recognized the dominions "as autonomous communities within the British Empire, equal

in status and in no way subordinate to one another in external affairs, united by a common allegiance to the crown". He was even happier when, at the 1931 conference, this declaration was incorporated in the Statute of Westminster and became the basis of the new British Commonwealth.

But Hertzog, in his turn, came to forfeit the confidence and trust of true Afrikaners. In 1933

Hertzog (left) and Smuts. In 1933 South Africa's two leading statesmen, previously Parliamentary opponents, came together to try to solve South Africa's growing economic problems. Their parties were "fused" in 1934 to form a new one: the United Party.

*This should not be confused with the Balfour Declaration of 1917 which proclaimed British support for a Jewish national home in Palestine.

he and most of his Nationalist followers made a political alliance with the South Africa Party of Smuts to form in 1934 the United Party. The occasion for this was the deepening world economic crisis and the need for a united approach to the problems it raised. In coming together, both parties modified part of their old political programmes. Hertzog abandoned his republicanism and generally adopted a more co-operative attitude towards Britain within the Commonwealth. Smuts agreed to give his support to two measures affecting Africans which Hertzog had for some time been anxious to pass. Believing in the need for a more thorough and logical application of segregation, Hertzog argued that the possession of the vote by even a limited number of Africans in the Cape was a threat to white supremacy. His view was in line with that of the South African Native Affairs Commission of 1903. He had been unable to change the position because of the entrenched clause which protected the voting rights of Africans in the Cape. But, with Smuts' support, he now had the necessary two-thirds majority in a joint session of the two houses of Parliament, and in 1936 the Representation of Natives Act was passed. It removed Africans in the Cape from the common electoral roll. In compensation, they were placed on a communal roll and elected three white representatives to the Assembly. Africans in the other three provinces together were to elect a total of four whites to represent them in the Senate. In addition, a Native Representative Council was set up, consisting of elected and nominated African members and white officials. Its powers were merely advisory.

Hertzog's second measure brought the hope of a slight improvement in the position of Africans with regard to land. The Native Trust and Land Act of 1936 provided for the transfer of 7¼ million morgen to the African reserves established in 1913. This was to take place over ten years. It was a step in the right direction; but it was too small a step. Moreover, like the recommendation of the Beaumont Commission in 1914, the provisions of this act were not implemented as planned because of white resistance to the transfer of any of their lands. Even twenty-five years after the act was passed, only a little over half of the promised additional land had been transferred.

The birth of the National Party

Hertzog's "fusion" with Smuts healed one breach between South African whites, but it also opened up new ones. In particular, a small group of Hertzog's Afrikaner Nationalists broke away, under the leadership of Dr D.F. Malan, an ex-predikant of the Dutch Reformed Church and later editor of the Afrikaner newspaper *Die Burger*. The group took the name of "Purified Nationalists". Though small at first, the new party inherited the mantle of guarding the true identity of the Afrikaner nation. As the National Party, they later won the election in 1948 and have governed South Africa ever since.

In the 1930s several other influences outside the political arena helped to bring about a great upsurge of Afrikaner Nationalism. The Dutch Reformed Church, always a powerful influence amongst Afrikaners, was one of these. Another was a secret society called the Broederbond. It had been founded in 1919 to promote, in every way possible, the identity and the interests of Afrikaners and to inspire in them a love of their language, their religion and their traditions. It was a select and dedicated body, whose members did their own recruiting on personal recommendation. They regarded themselves as the chosen of the chosen. Though they claimed no direct involvement in politics, they were committed to the advancement of Afrikanerdom in all spheres, and Hertzog and Smuts were both profoundly suspicious of their activities. In 1938 the Broederbond played a leading part in the plans for the centenary celebrations of Covenant Day. These took the form of a reconstruction of the events of the Great Trek, and reflected the Afrikaner's strong sense of history. They revived memories of the Afrikaners' struggle against the two enemies — the Africans and the British. The ox-wagon trek gathered momentum as it moved over the hallowed ground, covered a century earlier by the trekboers. It reached its climax at Pretoria where, as part of the ceremony, the foundation stone of the Voortrekker Monument was laid. The monument became the most important of the Holy Places of Afrikanerdom. It was completed in 1949, the year after the National Party came to power.

Between the enthusiasm and expectancy

generated by the celebrations in 1938 and the final triumph in the electoral victory in 1948, there came the Second World War. For Hertzog, the outbreak of war was the occasion which tested the reality of South Africa's independence from Britain. He wanted to keep South Africa neutral, and when his motion to do so was defeated in the House of Assembly, he resigned. Smuts became Prime Minister again and South Africa fought on the side of Britain. The Purified Nationalists and the Broederbond showed open sympathy for Germany. Some of them, including the future Prime Minister, B.J.Vorster, were arrested and imprisoned. For many, it was a disappointment when Hitler was eventually defeated. It seemed that Smuts was firmly in control and that power was still far beyond the reach of the Nationalists. In some ways, however, Smuts' growing stature in the international field prepared the way for his undoing. It seemed at times as if Smuts found South Africa's problems too trivial. His opponents were able to brand him more than ever as the friend of Britain and the "handyman of the Empire". But above all, as we have seen, his racial policy came under suspicion. In 1948 a nervous white electorate rejected him and turned to the National Party and the security promised by apartheid.

The Voortrekker Monument outside Pretoria. This is a national shrine for the Afrikaner people of South Africa. The foundations were laid during the centenary celebrations of the Battle of Blood River in 1938, and the opening ceremony was performed exactly eleven years later on 16 December 1949.

THE "NEW LOOK" OF APARTHEID UNDER THE NATIONALISTS

A more determined approach

It is sometimes argued that the essential features of South Africa's racial policy were so clearly defined before 1948 that apartheid was little more than a new name for an established system. Already Africans had been deprived of the little political power they had originally had in the Union. They were economically exploited. They were denied any permanent rights outside their reserves. All this continued under apartheid. Yet apartheid was much more than a change in name.

The Nationalists believed that, during and immediately after the Second World War, there had been a slow but dangerous erosion of the policy of segregation. For example, Africans had taken semi-skilled and skilled jobs; in increasing numbers, they were staying for longer periods in urban areas. Apartheid was the response of the Nationalists to these developments. It was also a response to a revolution in world opinion on racial questions, brought about by the Second World War. Contacts between people from different nations on a scale that had never happened before demolished the myth that the white races were superior to the coloured races. The Japanese had won massive victories over the white forces of Britain and the United States. Idealistic declarations by war leaders about human rights and the rights of people to self-determination sounded the death knell of colonialism. The achievement of independence by India in 1947 was the beginning of the long process of decolonization throughout the world. It was a process which gathered momentum with every success it won. Nationalist movements sprang up all over Africa. The two superpowers, the United States and Russia, encouraged the movement and were critical of colonialism as they vied with each other for the support of the peoples of Asia and Africa. White South Africans felt threatened by the stirrings of the black people to the north and by the new climate of world opinion. Before 1939 South Africa had been almost untouched by external pressures. From 1945 such pressures steadily grew. The South African government could not ignore them and they have undoubtedly influenced opinion and policies in South Africa.

In one respect, South Africa's response to these external pressures was the same as her response to developments at home. She tightened her racial policies and applied them with greater vigour. This tough reaction is one which can be detected over and over again since 1948. It was in marked contrast to the reaction of the leading colonial powers. Britain and France relaxed the colonial yoke and Britain openly acknowledged her intention of working towards the granting of self-government and then complete independence.

Yet, in another respect, apartheid has reflected an awareness of the critical attitude of the outside world. Perhaps the most striking difference between segregation before 1948 and apartheid after that date has been seen in the great efforts that the South African government has made to present apartheid to the world as a positive ideology. The emphasis has been on the concern to give to all the peoples of South Africa the chance to preserve their cultural identity, their way of life and their nationhood. Unfortunately, there is so much else about apartheid that is negative, so much that is blatantly discriminatory, so much that stands in the way of the interests of the non-white peoples and belies any claims of concern for their welfare, that these efforts of the South African government have been almost totally unsuccessful.

It is by studying the more important of the new laws that began to pour out from the South African parliament in 1948, that the new characteristics of apartheid can be seen. Such a study also soon makes it clear that apartheid was not a policy that had been worked out in detail before 1948. There were goals to be achieved and guidelines to be followed; but the means might have to be changed as circumstances and pressures changed. On one occasion, when Dr Malan, the first Nationalist Prime Minister, was being pressed by frustrated opponents to explain the difference between segregation and apartheid, he replied that there was no essential difference in their objectives. The difference lay in the fact that, under apartheid, the objectives were being pursued by a party that was united and determined to implement the policy as rapidly as possible.

Immorality Amendment Act, 1950

Thus, many of the new laws did little more than define earlier policies more clearly and attempt to enforce them more logically and systematically. Some of these laws operated at an individual level, such as the Prohibition of Mixed Marriages Act of 1949 and the Immorality Amendment Act of 1950. The original Immorality Act of 1927 had merely forbidden sexual intercourse between whites and Africans outside marriage. This permitted the purity of the races to be undermined legally. Under a system aimed at the separation of the races, it was illogical. The Amendment Act of 1950 was impossible to enforce as statistics have shown. The number of people convicted annually under the act has risen steadily and had topped the five-hundred mark by 1966. The difficulty of detecting the offence must mean that many more offenders go unidentified. Moreover, the distasteful methods adopted by the police to try to catch offenders help to explain why the police are unpopular. In this field of personal relationships, whites who become involved in offences are as resentful of apartheid as the non-whites.

Population Registration Act, 1950

It soon became obvious to the government that, if they intended to enforce their laws, the success of their efforts would often depend on the ability of the courts to identify the race of the parties involved. The Population Registration Act was therefore passed in 1950 and became one of the basic apartheid laws. Its object was to classify every South African into one of three racial categories: White, Coloured or Native. Later the Coloureds were sub-divided into Cape Coloureds,

The members of this family have become victims of the rigid application of apartheid. Pam is black; Abel is Coloured. They married and had children. The Group Areas Act made it illegal for them to live together as a family.

Malays, Chinese, Indian and other Asiatics. The measure and its application have illustrated the tragic consequences of apartheid. The Coloureds are the most difficult category to identify. Some of the children of mixed marriages can be indistinguishable from whites; others indistinguishable from blacks. Not surprisingly, cases of re-classification in the light of new information are common. The law has led to cruel situations resulting from the splitting up of families.

Group Areas Act, 1950

Other laws operate at group or community level. The most important and fundamental of these is probably the Group Areas Act, 1950. The Prime Minister Dr Malan, speaking of the measure, said: "What we have in this Bill is apartheid. It is the essence of apartheid policy which is embodied in this Bill." It was the National government's way of dealing with the great contradiction which has always been at the heart of segregation and apartheid: the presence in the white areas of South Africa, especially in urban areas, of large numbers of non-whites. Today (1980) well over 60 per cent of the black population of South Africa lives outside the reserves or homelands. No town or city in South Africa has a white majority. This is a situation which makes nonsense of any claims that apartheid can be logically and absolutely applied.

The Native Urban Areas Act of 1923 (see page 25) had been optional. Its adoption by smaller local authorities was slow and its implementation patchy. Many were reluctant to subsidize African housing. Conditions in African locations often remained a disgrace. The Nationalists showed typical vigour and ruthlessness in tackling the problem. Separate residential and ownership areas were designated throughout the country by the Group Areas Board for all four main racial groups. The act had more devastating results for a large number of people than any other single apartheid measure. It necessitated the uprooting and movement of whole communities. Although far more Africans were affected than members of any other race, Asians too, with much urban property and wide trading interests, stood to lose a great deal. In general, it meant that non-whites would be compulsorily moved from inner suburbs of cities and towns all over the country. Their titles to any property they might hold there would lapse. What happened to Africans all over the country happened also to Coloureds mainly in Cape Town and to Indians mainly in Durban.

One such exercise in the uprooting of an established community concerned the township of Sophiatown, about four miles from the centre of Johannesburg. The story of its "removal" in 1955 to a new "location" at Meadowlands, further out of the city, is worth telling in some detail, because it illustrates the National government's methods and determination to sweep aside opposition to its will. The story also attracted international attention, because the people of Sophiatown were served by Father Trevor Huddleston, an Anglican priest, who took up their cause.

Sophiatown was a rather special township. It was not a soul-destroying, municipal-owned location, with plot upon plot of almost uniform little boxes. It had a pleasant situation on a rocky ridge on the western fringe of the city. Most important of all, many of its people owned their own plots and their own homes. They were free-holders, a rare status for Africans. It was also a

Sophiatown. Before the Group Areas Act this road divided Sophiatown, home of many black Africans and other non-whites, from the newer white suburb of Westdene on the western outskirts of Johannesburg. After the act the whole area was designated white, Sophiatown was destroyed and its inhabitants moved to a new township.

mixed township for, though most of its people were Africans, there were others. Its cosmopolitan character was an affront to the spirit of apartheid and the Group Areas Act. To Father Huddleston, who went there in 1943, it was a lively, happy community that deserved to be saved. He wrote about it with affection in his book *Naught For Your Comfort*:

> Its dusty, dirty streets and its slovenly shops, its sprawling and unplanned stretches of corrugated iron roof: its foetid and insanitary yards? ". . . and the streets of the city shall be full of boys and girls playing in the streets thereof . . . " is a description of the heavenly Jerusalem. It is a good one. And anyone who has lived as I have in that "slum" called Sophiatown will recognize how swiftly, through the presence of its children and through their unspoilt and unassailable laughter, Heaven can break in upon this old and dreary world.
>
> I have said that Sophiatown is a gay place. It is more. It has a vitality and an exuberance about it which belong to no other suburb in South Africa: certainly to no white suburb. It positively sparkles with life . . . . (Trevor Huddleston, *Naught For Your Comfort*, Collins, London, 1956, p.132-3.)

By 1944 Sophiatown was tumble-down, squalid and very overcrowded, though not more so than many other locations around Johannesburg. It was officially a slum. Its overcrowding was due largely to the failure of Johannesburg's City Council to build homes for the thousands of African workers who had poured into the city in the late '30s and early '40s, to supply the labour for its mines and factories. Sophiatown's real crime, however, was that it had become a "black spot" among the white suburbs which were encroaching on its borders. It had existed long before whites had begun to regard this part of the city as a pleasant residential area. In 1939 the first European demands were made for the removal of Sophiatown and other nearby locations. In 1944 the City Council agreed in principle to their removal. Nothing was done, however, and the government of the day, Smuts's United Party government, did not intervene.

Shanty towns began to mushroom round the western fringe of the city.

With the arrival in power of Malan's Nationalist government and the passing of the Group Areas Act, Sophiatown was seriously threatened. The City Council was ordered to implement its 1944 proposals. In 1953 Father Huddleston became the chairman of the Western Areas Protest Committee, whose object was to persuade the City Council not to co-operate with the government. It succeeded. But this was a government not to be diverted from its purpose. It believed in the rightness of what it was doing. It thought it knew better than the campaign committee or the people of Sophiatown. Dr Verwoerd, the Minister of Native Affairs, created a new local authority and ordered it to carry out his plans. He conducted a very successful propaganda campaign, accusing all who opposed the plans of obstructing much-needed slum clearance. Father Huddleston knew that this was dishonest and that the real reason for destroying Sophiatown was not the clearing of slums. He wrote:

> Basically the issue was dead simple. It was just this: that white Johannesburg had encroached on black Johannesburg, and so, naturally, black Johannesburg must move on. MUST MOVE ON . . . . An African freehold township, established for 50 years, can be uprooted and totally destroyed because it is contiguous with a European suburb. The question of right or wrong does not have any relevance (Trevor Huddleston, op. cit., p. 186-188.)

The end for Sophiatown came with ruthless efficiency and suddenness. Before dawn on 10 February 1955, two days before the scheduled date, a large force of police and soldiers arrived, armed to the teeth and with a fleet of military lorries in attendance, to move the people of Sophiatown to the new location of Meadowlands. Father Huddleston believed that the destruction of Sophiatown was "a loss immeasurable":

> The truth is that Sophiatown is a community: a living organism which has grown up through the years, and which has struck its roots deep

in this particular place and in this special soil. (Trevor Huddleston, op. cit., p. 134.)

Pass laws

In the years before the Second World War nothing had aroused more resentment amongst Africans than the pass laws. Chief Albert Luthuli, one of the main African leaders in the 1950s, wrote this about them:

> It cannot be easy for you to understand the very deep hatred all Africans feel for a pass. Can anyone who has not been through it possibly imagine what has happened when they read in the press of a routine police announcement that there has been a raid on a location . . . .
>
> Each year half a million of my people are arrested under the pass laws. The physical act of detention with the consequence of a broken home, a lost job, a loss of earnings is only part of this grim picture. The deep humiliation felt by a black man . . . when over again he hears the shout "Kaffir, where's your pass?" fills the rest of the picture.

The pass laws have been essential to the operation of segregation and apartheid. They made it possible for the government to know the place of every African. They have been the means by which the police can tell instantly, by demanding to see an African's pass, whether he is in his proper place. His "proper place", unless he has a permit to be elsewhere and this is recorded in his pass, is on the reserve.

In 1952 the government passed a measure curiously and misleadingly named the Abolition of Passes and Co-ordination of Documents Act. From this date, all Africans had to carry reference books. The reference book contained detailed information about the bearer in a single document instead of in several different ones. The reference book is a pass, in spite of the title of the act which introduced the new system. Nelson Mandela found this act a good illustration of Nationalist tactics:

> It is typical of the Nationalists' propaganda

The pass "book" is bitterly resented as the symbol of the second-class status of Africans.

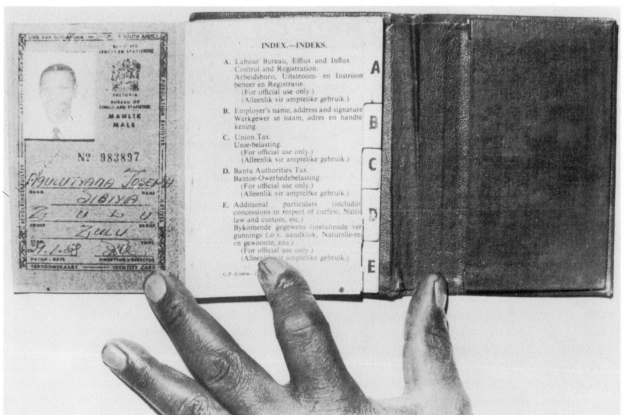

Pass burning. The persistence and frequency of demonstrations against the pass laws are a measure of the strong feelings which these laws arouse. The burning of passes by blacks has been a regular form of protest against apartheid.

The arrest of an African whose pass was found to be not in order. ►

techniques that they describe their measures in misleading titles, which convey the opposite of what the measures contain. Verwoerd called his law greatly extending and intensifying the pass laws the 'Abolition of Passes' Act.

The 1952 act also illustrates the tightening up of the race laws under apartheid. In 1942 the United Party Minister of Native Affairs had condemned the pass laws. They were the cause of over a quarter of a million arrests and convictions annually in the Transvaal. A relaxation of their operation followed until the Nationalists came to power. The 1952 act was a clear sign of the return to strict enforcement. Not surprisingly, the continued obligation to carry reference books became the commonest cause of African protest. Offences under the law continued to grow. In the twenty-five years between 1948 and 1973, well over ten million Africans were arrested because their passes were not in order.

"Petty" apartheid

It has often been said that the Afrikaner is more logical over racial issues than the English-speaking South African, and that this logical streak shows in much of the legislation passed by the Afrikaner-dominated National Party. For example, in 1953

A fine beach, reserved for whites only, on the Atlantic coast of the Cape peninsula. This is an example of "petty" apartheid. The law requires that local authorities, in many public places, shall provide "separate but not necessarily equal" amenities for whites and non-whites.

the Preservation of Separate Amenities Act applied the principle of the separation of the races to a wide variety of situations in everyday life. It legalized the irritating and humiliating system of "petty" apartheid. In most public places separate "but not necessarily equal" amenities were provided for non-whites and whites. The familiar notices in English and Afrikaans became a common sight everywhere in South Africa. "Whites only" or "Net blankes"; "Non-whites" or "Nie Blankes" appeared on park benches, in banks, railway stations, post offices, in sports grounds, outside toilets, restaurants and places of entertainment.

The Separate Representation of Voters Bill

It was also illogical that Coloured voters should still be enrolled on the common voters' roll in Cape Province. Africans had been removed from the roll in 1936 by Hertzog's Representation of Voters Act. In 1949 the Natives Representative Council had been abolished. In 1951 Dr Malan, in the Separate Representation of Voters Bill, tried to remove the last of the non-

white voters from the common roll — the Coloureds. The measure was passed, but was declared invalid by the Supreme Court because it had not received the two-thirds majority in a joint session of the two houses of parliament required by the entrenched clauses in the South Africa Act. Eventually, under Malan's successor, J.G. Strijdom, the bill was made valid, but only after a prolonged and bitter constitutional crisis and the use by the government of the doubtful devices of appointing new judges and packing an enlarged Senate with Nationalist supporters.

This measure finally established in South Africa what the delegates from the Transvaal, the Orange Free State and Natal had wanted when the Union constitution was being drawn up between 1908 and 1910: an exclusively white franchise for the election of the country's Parliament. The Nationalist government could claim that this was more logical and more justifiable in 1951 than it would have been in 1910. They had, after all, announced their intention of giving political rights to Africans in their own homelands. It was no longer reasonable that they should also have political rights in what the Nationalists claimed was "White South Africa". It was all part of the more positive side of Nationalist racial policy, the "new look" of apartheid.

THE BANTUSTANS

The more positive, ideological elements in apartheid, as seen by the National Party, were set out in a series of measures which should eventually lead to the establishment of a group of Bantu "homelands" or "Bantustans" for the several so-called Bantu "nations" living in South Africa. The first two of these measures were passed in 1951 and 1959. It needs to be emphasized that the basis of this policy is mythical. It rests on the untenable view that the old reserves, established in 1913, had been the homes of the Bantu-speaking "tribes" since their arrival in the country at a date little earlier than that of the arrival of the first Dutch settlers at the Cape. We have seen (page 7) that the Bantu-speakers arrived many centuries before this and that, long before the Great Trek and the Mfecane changed the pattern of settlement in South Africa, they had occupied many parts of what is now claimed as "white" South Africa.

The policy has been particularly associated with Dr Heinrich F. Verwoerd, who was Minister of Native Affairs from 1950 to 1958 and Prime Minister from 1958 to 1966. He was one of the architects of apartheid. He had been a brilliant scholar and had studied first at the Afrikaner University of Stellenbosch and later at several German Universities before returning to a Professorship in Psychology at Stellenbosch. He left academic life to become editor of *Die Transvaaler*, one of the more extreme Nationalist newspapers. He moved into politics in 1948.

The Party's election manifesto and the Sauer Report (see page 28) had outlined the Nationalists' plans for making the reserves the "national" homes of the different Bantu-speaking peoples. Here the Africans would be able to develop along their own lines and preserve their culture and traditional way of life. The whites would be the guardians of their interests. "We grant to the Bantu what we demand for ourselves — the right to preserve our culture and inheritance — and develop our potential to the full."

The National Party plans were further spelled out in 1951 in the Bantu Authorities Act. This act made it clear that the government intended to establish tribal authorities in the reserves, as the basis of eventual self-government in their homelands. In answer to a question about whether there might one day be complete independence for these African homelands, however, Malan in 1950 seemed to rule out the possibility:

It stands to reason that white South Africa must remain their guardian . . . . The areas will be economically dependent on the Union . . . . It stands to reason where we talk of Natives' right of self-government in those areas we cannot mean that we intend to cut large slices out of South Africa and turn them into independent states.

Dr Eiselen, another of the architects of apartheid, said much the same thing:

The utmost degree of autonomy which the Union Parliament is likely to be prepared to concede to these areas will stop short of actual surrender of sovereignty by the European trustee.

The claims made for the new policy that it satisfied the national aspirations of both the whites and other racial groups were not true. For the Coloureds and the Asians, there was the inescapable fact that they had no reserves and therefore no "homelands". The leaders of the African National Congress made it very clear that they rejected these plans. As Professor Edgar Brooke, a senator and one of the persistent critics of apartheid, pointed out: the African would "develop along his own lines" but the Nationalist government would tell him what those lines should be. The Africans were never consulted about the plans.

Ironically, the tribal institutions which were to be set up in the homelands had long since been undermined by white policies. Tribal societies had been torn apart under economic pressures, not least by the drastic reduction in the amount of land available for African use. The Africans with the greatest political awareness were those in the urban areas, who were the most completely detribalized. They were increasing in number in spite of Nationalist policy. More of them were permanent or at least "permanent-temporary" residents in the towns and cities. It is worth noting that, when, in 1952, the ANC announced its intention of opposing the "six unjust laws", the Bantu Authorities Act was included in the list.

The Tomlinson Commission

In announcing its plans for the homelands, the government seemed to show that it was serious by appointing a commission, under Professor Tomlinson, to make recommendations for their economic and social development. The Tomlinson Commission issued its report in 1954. It was a thorough piece of work in seventeen massive volumes. It warned the government that urgent consideration would have to be given to the economic development of the reserves if they were to have any chance of fulfilling the role mapped out for them. The report recommended that £104 million should be spent in the first ten years of a twenty-five-year plan. Given this investment, it might be possible for the homelands to provide homes for 15 million Africans by the year 2000. By this date, however, the projected African population would be some 21½ million. The report also recommended the extension and the consolidation of the reserves, realizing that their scattered, fragmented nature made them unsuitable as national homes. It hoped that the three British High Commission Territories, the British protectorates of Basutoland, Bechuanaland and Swaziland, which Britain had excluded from the Union in 1910, might soon be incorporated. Their area would make the total area of the homelands look vastly more respectable,

expressed as a percentage of the total area of South Africa. In fact, however, it was becoming less and less likely that Britain would allow this to happen, as South Africa's racial policies hardened under apartheid.

The Nationalist government virtually ignored the clear and urgent recommendations of its commission. This threw the gravest doubts on the ideological and high-sounding claims it had been making for its policy of self-governing homelands capable of supporting more and more Africans. For, without the sort of investment advised by Tomlinson, the reserves would not be able to support, at a reasonable living standard, even those Africans already living there, let alone additional Africans, who had been removed, under apartheid, from the urban areas, or who were part of the predicted increase in population.

The Bantu Education Act, 1953

The African's life was also to be reorganized on the basis of another report: that of the Eiselen Commission on Native Education. Appointed in 1949, this Commission reported in 1951. The report, at least by implication, was critical of the education previously given to African children. Almost all of it had been provided in mission schools. There were, however, some contradictions in the report. At one point it stated:

> The Bantu child comes to school with a basic physical and psychological endowment which differs so slightly if at all from that of the European child that no special provision has to be made in educational theory or basic aims.

Yet it also stated that the education given to the European was quite unsuitable for the African. The overall message was clear enough: Bantu education must be changed. It must become an integral part of the wider plan for Bantu development. It must help to preserve the Bantu cultural inheritance and take into account the current stage of their development. The Bantu Education Act of 1953 brought the education of Africans directly under the control of the Ministry of Bantu Affairs. Bantu education was to become an instrument of government policy. "Education

Two Bantu schools, in the country (top) and in Soweto (left). The Bantu Education Act of 1953 introduced a separate system of education, under government control, for the black people of South Africa. Money spent on Bantu education is only a fraction of that spent on white education and it can hardly be denied that the former is an inferior product.

must be co-ordinated into a definite and carefully planned policy for the development of Bantu societies."

Statements made by Dr Verwoerd, the Minister concerned, leave little doubt about the real purpose of the act and its consequences for Bantu education. The report, for example, had stated: "The aims of Bantu education are the development of character and intellect, and the equipping of the child for his future work and surroundings". Nobody could take exception to that. However, Dr Verwoerd said: "The school must equip him

[the African] to meet the demands which the economic life of South Africa *will impose upon him* . . . . There is no place for the native in European society above the level of certain forms of labour." The education so far provided for natives had given them dangerous notions. It had given them ambition. "Race relations cannot improve if the wrong sort of education is given to the Africans; if the result of education is the creation of frustrated people; when it creates people who are trained for professions not open to them." This must change. "The Bantu teacher must be integrated as an active agent in the process of the development of the Bantu community. He must learn not to feel above his community with a consequent desire to become integrated into the life of the European community."

The Africans might be forgiven for believing that they were being offered a limited, second-rate form of education. Father Huddleston's comment on the new education was:

It is indeed an education for servitude. But it has come too late. It has come when, after more than a century of Christian education, the door is already open to a wider and freer world of vision. It will take more than Dr Verwoerd to close that door.

In 1976 rioting was sparked off in Soweto by an educational issue: the African's resentment of the fact that part of his instruction must be given in Afrikaans, a language which is foreign to him and is the language of his oppressors.

The Extension of University Education Act, 1959

In 1959, in the Extension of University Education Act, it was the turn of higher education to be brought into line with apartheid. This is another example of a measure which was given a misleading title. It is true that it led to the establishment of two new colleges for Africans, one in the northern Transvaal and the other in Zululand. The old college at Fort Hare in Natal was turned into an ethnic college for the Xhosa people. But previously, African students had attended the open universities of Cape Town and the Witwatersrand, along with white students. In future, non-white students would be admitted to these institutions only in special circumstances and with government permission. A commission of inquiry had ruled that the attendance of Africans at open universities would "give students a background which does not fit in with their national character and will give them an alien and contemptuous attitude towards their own culture". It was recommended that, in future, each college or university should serve one ethnic group and that the products of these colleges should find their highest fulfilment in the enrichment of their own social groups.

In spite of government assurances to the contrary, these "bush" universities, as they have come to be called, have not attained the same academic standards as the white universities. They have not been given international recognition. Their establishment has wasted scarce resources. They have not attracted as many students as was hoped and they have not become the nuclei for urban development within the homelands. An African lecturer at one of them, the University of Zululand, stated in 1979:

> The students have nothing else, therefore they tolerate the university but do not accept it. This university is the product of a political system and we are deeply suspicious of it. If the white universities were opened to blacks, most of us would prefer to go there.

The Promotion of Bantu Self-Government Act, 1959

The government's refusal to act on the advice of the Tomlinson Commission did not stop it going ahead in 1959 with the next step in its programme for developing the homelands. The Promotion of Bantu Self-Government Act provided for the setting up of eight national territorial units, since increased to ten, based on the country's main tribal groups. These groups were, with the names of the corresponding Bantustans added in brackets: the North Sotho (Lebowa); the South Sotho (Qwaqwa); the Tswana (Bophuthatswana); the Zulu (Kwazulu); the Swazi (Swazi); the Xhosa (Transkei and Ciskei); and the Venda (Venda). A white Commissioner

In 1959 the principle of apartheid was applied to higher education by the Extension of Universities Act. This photograph shows part of the University of the North at Turfloop in the Northern Transvaal. It is a fine campus but, given the opportunity, Africans would prefer to go to an "open" University.

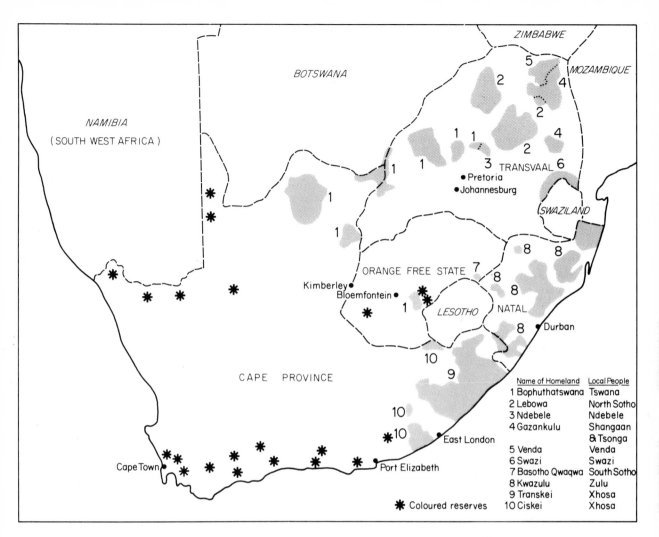

The proposed Bantu homelands or Bantustans.

Name of Homeland	Local People
1 Bophuthatswana	Tswana
2 Lebowa	North Sotho
3 Ndebele	Ndebele
4 Gazankulu	Shangaan & Tsonga
5 Venda	Venda
6 Swazi	Swazi
7 Basotho Qwaqwa	South Sotho
8 Kwazulu	Zulu
9 Transkei	Xhosa
10 Ciskei	Xhosa

✳ Coloured reserves

General would be appointed to guide each national unit. The territorial legislatures would be given limited powers, but a veto would remain with the South African government over the appointment of chiefs and over any legislation which it disliked.

Dr Verwoerd said that an increasing measure of self-government would be granted to the territories as progress was made and eventually, perhaps, complete independence. In 1960 a spokesman for the government interpreted Dr Verwoerd's policy as "having in view for the Native people in their areas the same benefits in every way as for the whites in their areas — including eventual sovereign independence". Dr Verwoerd said that, when this happened, the Bantustans would still remain economically dependent on South Africa and he envisaged the development of some sort of Commonwealth of Southern African states. At this time he tried to tempt the British High Commission Territories into association with South Africa by offering them the prospect of independence on the new South African model rather than on the British pattern. He pointed to what he believed to be some superior features of the South African Bantustan. Europeans would be excluded, whereas Britain was leading its territories to an independence on a multi-racial basis where whites would possess political powers alongside Africans. The peoples of the three territories, however, refused to be tempted.

When confronted with the challenge that the Africans themselves had not been consulted about the new proposals, Dr Verwoerd was

Contrast in the Transkei. Above: a new industrial town in the southern Transkei — an all too rare example of industrial development inside a Bantustan. Below: a typical rural scene in the Transkei showing traditional Xhosa homes.

remarkably frank. The bill, he said, was really concerned with the preservation of white dominance, and the government was "not prepared to call in the Bantu" on such a measure. At times the Prime Minister was capable of making statements which could hardly be reconciled with his more ideological claims. The measure also ended the last indirect representation for Africans in the South African Parliament. The three whites representing Cape Africans in the Assembly and the four whites representing Africans in the rest of the Union in the Senate would no longer be justified once Africans had political rights in their homelands. The Africans regarded the act as a means of dividing and weakening them on a tribal basis.

A Bantu Investment Corporation was set up to encourage and assist in the establishment of business and industry in the homelands. The £500,000 capital allocated to the corporation seemed an irrelevant token gesture when set against the recommendations of the Tomlinson Commission five years earlier. Nelson Mandela, one of the main leaders of the ANC, wrote that the policy outlined in the act was designed to "help the Nationalists perpetrate a fraud".

The Bantustans in practice

The first of the new homelands was established in 1963 by the Transkei Constitution Act. The Transkei was by far the most compact and the most viable of the proposed states. Most of them were small, fragmented and scattered. Their leaders have repeatedly called for the addition of more land, and in 1973 the government made further proposals for consolidation. The previous proposals in 1936, however, had still not been implemented in full and prospects were not good.

A further landmark in the implementation of the plan came in 1976 when the Transkei was granted so-called independence. In theory, at least, and in a shorter time than had been anticipated from ministerial speeches, Verwoerd's promise of independence was fulfilled. In 1978 Bophuthatswana and in 1979 Venda achieved the same status.

One setback for the government's plans has been the refusal of Chief Buthelezi, chief Minister of Kwazulu, to accept independence for his people, on the grounds that, to do so, would be to give the stamp of approval to the policy. He had accepted the policy so far because it was the only way that blacks could find any means of political expression. Any other approach would have led to "detentions, Robben Island [the government's maximum security prison for political prisoners] and even the noose".

The rest of the world remained sceptical about the genuineness of the independence offered to the homelands and refused to recognize the new states. The newly named "Bantustans" were still fulfilling the same function as the old reserves: they are reservoirs of cheap labour for the white economy. They are also dumping grounds for Africans who, for one reason or another, are no longer needed in "white" South Africa. Such Africans are returned to the "Ban-

tustans" even though it has become impossible to allocate many of them to a particular "homeland" or "black nation" after years of mixing and detribalization in an urban environment. One writer has put it this way: the policy of "apartheid" "is essentially one of maintaining a delicate balance in the distribution of the African population. Those who are needed stay where they are needed; those who are not stay in the reserves. The restriction of Africans to legal residence in the Bantustans is basic to the whole working of the economic system".

So far, therefore, Dr Verwoerd's loudly proclaimed "supremely positive step" in the apartheid programme has not persuaded opinion outside South Africa that the policy is anything other than a new way of exploiting the African inhabitants of the country. To the outside world, and to the real leaders of African Nationalism, South Africa remains a single country which denies political rights to the majority of its inhabitants.

Chief Buthelezi, Chief Minister of the Zulu homeland of Kwazulu, visiting an old Zulu woman. Among black leaders in South Africa today, he is a moderate and an opponent of violence. But he disapproves of apartheid and accepts some of what it offers under protest and as a temporary measure.

AFRICAN REACTIONS TO APARTHEID 1948~1960

One important group of new measures has so far not been mentioned. These are the measures, passed from 1950 onwards, designed to suppress opposition. The Nationalist government's determination to enforce apartheid bred a more active and eventually a more violent response from Africans. A vicious circle of protest and new repressive legislation was soon started.

The organizations representing the non-white races were the African National Congress (ANC); the Indian National Congress (INC); and the Coloured People's Congress (CPC). Since its foundation in 1912, the ANC had been narrowly based on the educated African elite and had always conducted its fight for African rights in a constitutional and peaceful manner. Its appeal had been to the good sense of liberal whites who had shown sympathy with African aspirations for participation in a multi-racial state practising no discrimination. In 1943 a Youth League was established which called for more militant action, and in 1949 the ANC decided that the time for action had arrived and planned a programme of strikes and civil disobedience. In 1950 there was rioting, and the ANC called upon workers to stay away from work on 1 May in a "Freedom Day" protest. In June the government passed what was probably the greatest of all its repressive measures, the Suppression of Communism Act. The act contained a definition of communism so broad that it embraced almost any act of opposition against the government. This "statutory" communism was the government's most widely used weapon against its opponents.

By 1951 the ANC and the INC were co-ordinating their protests against apartheid, and in 1952 the ANC announced its intention of embarking upon a "Defiance Campaign" on 26 June, unless the government had before that date repealed a group of six unjust laws, which included the Suppression of Communism Act, the Group Areas Act and the Bantu Authorities Act. A letter signed by the President and Secretary of the ANC gave the government warning of their plans. The government ignored the warning and the act of defiance began. The commonest form of action was to ignore "petty" apartheid signs. By October five thousand Africans had been arrested and the demonstrations had become violent. Moreover, the ANC was clearly trying to broaden its appeal and to become a mass movement, like the nationalist movements in colonial territories to the north. The government was worried by the new tactics, but the number of people arrested was not large enough to exceed the capacity of the prisons. Early in 1953 the Criminal Law Amendment Act armed the forces of law and order with additional powers. Punishments were severe and included the liberal use of the lash, a feature which earned the new measure the tital of "the whipping post bill". The Defiance Campaign ended. Brutal repression had achieved its purpose. To emphasize its determination to enforce its policy, the government passed the Reservation of Separate Amenities Act. The leadership of the non-white congress movements was weakened by the many arrests under the Suppression of Communism Act.

The ANC, however, remained firm in its resolve to reject violence as a method of fighting apartheid. This was confirmed by Albert Luthuli, the new leader of the movement, in 1953. Late in the previous year Luthuli, chief of a small tribe in Natal, had been deposed from his chieftaincy by the government. He had been supporting the Defiance Campaign, and the government gave him the choice of resigning either from his chieftaincy or from the ANC. He chose the former, and used the occasion to issue a statement in which he summarized his career in public life and his struggle for African rights:

The prelude to the Defiance Campaign. The ANC called for the repeal of the "six unjust laws" before the end of February 1952. Otherwise they threatened a large-scale disobedience campaign.

Who will deny that 30 years of my life have been spent knocking in vain, patiently, moderately and modestly at a closed barred door? What have been the fruits of moderation? The past 30 years have seen the greatest number of laws restricting our rights and progress, until we have reached a stage where we have almost no rights at all . . . . I have embraced the non-violent Passive Resistance technique in fighting for freedom because I am convinced it is the only non-revolutionary, legitimate and humane way that could be used by people denied effective constitutional means.

In spite of continuing frustrations, Luthuli never wavered in his twin commitment to non-violence and a non-racial society.

In the atmosphere of the years 1954-58 others were less patient and less sure of the rightness and effectiveness of Luthuli's methods. The Prime Minister during these years was J.G. Strijdom, a hard, uncompromising Transvaaler, nicknamed "the lion of the north". It was a period of mounting repression. Tough and often brutal police methods contributed to the worsening race relations. In Parliament in 1955 the Prime Minister spoke plainly about his policy:

Call it paramountcy, *baaskap* or what you will, it is still domination. I am being as blunt as I can. Either the white man dominates or the

The Defiance Campaign. An ANC leader appealing to Africans in Freedom Square, Johannesburg, to support the Defiance Campaign called for 26 June 1952. It was the first militant campaign planned by the previously law-abiding movement.

black man takes over . . . . The government of the country is in the hands of the white man because of the franchise laws and for that reason the white man is *baas* in South Africa.

In the same year delegates from the non-white congresses and representatives of white opposition groups met at a Congress of the People and adopted the "Freedom Charter". The charter asserted that "South Africa belongs to all who live in it, Black and White". It called for equal rights for all, including voting rights; and the repeal of apartheid laws.

These years marked the height of the multi-racial campaign against apartheid, and three white opposition groups were active. These were the Torch Commando, the Women's Defence of the Constitution League, and the Federation of South African Women. The first two fought the attempt to disfranchise Coloured voters, and the

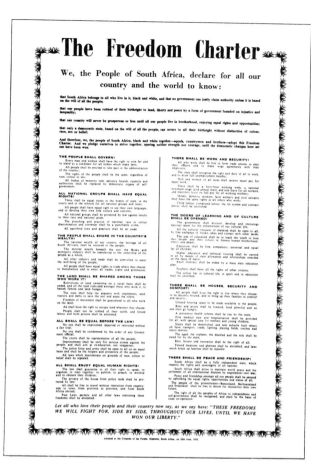

The Freedom Charter. A multi-racial "Congress of the People" met at Kliptown near Johannesburg in 1955 and drew up the "Freedom Charter" which called for an end to apartheid.

Luthuli (above) and Sobukwe (below). Two African leaders who disagreed about tactics. Chief Albert Luthuli, President of the ANC after 1953, refused to depart from the principles of non-violence and non-racialism. Robert Sobukwe, a much younger man, founded the break-away Pan-Africanist Congress in 1958 which was committed to neither.

last opposed the extension of the pass laws to women. In December 1956, 156 of the government's leading opponents from these and the non-white organizations were suddenly arrested. They were charged with treason and offences under the Suppression of Communism Act. The trial, known as the Treason Trial, dragged on until March 1961, when the last twenty-eight defendants were all acquitted. The trial had attracted world-wide interest and concentrated much publicity, along with other events in 1960-61, on South Africa's race policies.

Strijdom died in 1958. In the same year, growing disillusionment at the failure of the campaign against apartheid led to the foundation by Robert Sobukwe of the Pan Africanist Congress (PAC). The new movement was partly inspired by the successes of the nationalist movements in many African countries against colonial

rule, particularly in Ghana where independence was gained from Britain in 1957. In two ways the PAC differed from the ANC. It was not committed to non-violence and it believed that Africans must fight their own battles. It did not favour the ANC's policy of working with the other congress movements and white opposition groups in the Congress Alliance formed in 1954. It stressed the need for Africans, initially at least, to gain self confidence and self-respect.

In the year of the PAC's foundation Dr Verwoerd became Prime Minister. Under his decisive leadership, efforts were made to give substance to the more positive image of apartheid. He had an overwhelming belief in the destiny of the Afrikaner people, in the rightness of Nationalist policy, and in the possibility that it could be made to work. The years of his premiership were a period of returning confidence for South African whites in general and for

The Cato Manor disturbances, 1959. Violent protests by black Africans became more common in the late 1950s, as in the township of Cato Manor outside Durban. Here, in a demonstration mainly by women against the liquor laws, a beer hall was sacked and vehicles were set on fire.

Afrikaners in particular. He lost no time in switching away from the almost totally negative and defensive policy of Strijdom to a policy designed to enable South Africa to pass to the offensive. Measures like the Promotion of Bantu Self-Government Act and the Extension of University Education Act were given titles in keeping with the new approach.

A tough line was still taken against any opposition, and demonstrations became more, rather than less, frequent. One of the most serious took place in the township of Cato Manor outside Durban, where a protest led by women against the hated liquor laws erupted into violence. The liquor laws were almost as fertile a cause of

African protest as the pass laws. To brew and sell illicit beer was one of the traditional ways in which African women could eke out a precarious existence. In Cato Manor they boycotted the municipal beer halls and reacted violently to police interference.

Early in 1960 two significant events took place. In February, Harold Macmillan, the British Prime Minister, made his famous "wind of change" speech at the end of his African tour, in the Parliament at Cape Town. He declared that Britain could not approve of South Africa's race policies and might soon have to choose between good relations with 200 million black Africans or with 4 million white South Africans. The speech was resented and hardened white attitudes. A few weeks later Verwoerd said in Parliament: "The white man of Africa is not going to be told that, because he is outnumbered by the black people, he must allow his rights to be swallowed up."

In March 1960 the PAC planned what proved to be its first and last demonstration, a passive resistance campaign during which Africans were to destroy their passes and offer themselves for arrest at police stations. On 21 March, at Sharpeville, a township near Vereeniging, nervous police opened fire on a large, excited, but unarmed and peaceful crowd. It was generally believed that the police opened fire unnecessarily. Sixty-seven Africans were killed and 186 wounded. Most of them had been shot in the back while running away. The news echoed round the world.

Sharpeville massacre. Here in March 1960 a demonstration organized by the PAC against the pass laws ended in tragedy when police fired on an African crowd, killing 67 and injuring about 180. The episode provoked world-wide condemnation of South Africa's apartheid policy.

AFRICAN REACTIONS TO APARTHEID 1960~1976

The South African government was shaken by Sharpeville and by world reaction to it. A few days later it was temporarily deprived of its leader when Dr Verwoerd was shot and injured by a white farmer of deranged mind. For a moment it seemed as though the government was about to reconsider its policies. The Acting-Prime Minister said:

> The old book of South African history was closed a month ago and, for the immediate future, South Africa will reconsider in earnest and honestly her whole approach to the Native question. We must create a new spirit which must restore overseas faith — both white and non-white in South Africa.

But Verwoerd recovered. His recovery was seen as the hand of God at work for His chosen people. A few minor concessions were made including the abolition of the liquor laws, but the whole policy of "separate development", as Verwoerd now preferred to call it, was re-affirmed. In October 1960 Verwoerd held a referendum in which the whites were asked whether they wanted South Africa to become a republic. It was a revival of the old Afrikaner policy which had been a priority in the heady days of the centenary celebrations of the Battle of Blood River in 1938 (see page 13). But little had been heard of it since 1948. Verwoerd won the majority he wanted by 70,000 votes and Republic Day was fixed for 31 May 1961.

Before it arrived, South Africa had left the Commonwealth. When Verwoerd attended the Commonwealth Conference in London in March 1961, he was so "shocked by the spirit of hostility and victimization shown to South Africa" that he withdrew the application for continued membership that he had made. Macmillan said that South Africa had been condemned because her apartheid theory "transposes what we regard as wrong into right". South Africa's withdrawal from the Commonwealth was unpopular with many English speakers and with Africans; and Nelson Mandela, now their main leader, called for a three-day stay-at-home leading up to Republic Day. The results of this last major attempt at organized political protest were disappointing. Another General Law Amendment Act gave the authorities power to hold suspects for twelve days instead of forty-eight hours.

For the next three years a short-lived campaign of violent protest was waged by two new movements — the Spear of the Nation, generally supposed to be associated with the ANC, and POQO, a successor movement to the PAC. The two old movements had been banned after Sharpeville. Sabotage was the weapon of the new campaign. Predictably, the government strengthened its defences. Vast sums were spent on the armed forces, ostensibly to meet the mounting communist threat. Sabotage was made a capital offence. Under General Law Amendment Acts suspects could be held for ninety days without charge (later extended to 180 days). House arrest was added to the various banning possibilities, to deal with people who could not be condemned in a court of law. Mass trials became common. Nelson Mandela, who had come to be called the "Black Pimpernel", for his skill in evading arrest, was caught in August 1962 and in the following year an informer betrayed the headquarters of the Spear of the Nation in Rivonia, a suburb of Johannesburg. The Rivonia trial followed, with Mandela the main defendant. He conducted his own defence, and skilfully used the trial as a platform to publicize the plight of South Africa's blacks. In his closing speech he eloquently reviewed the struggle of Africans for "the right to live":

> Africans want to be paid a living wage. Africans

MANDELA'S DEFENCE

On November 8, Nelson Mandela, South Africa's "Black Pimpernel," was sent to prison for five years—three for inciting people to strike and two for leaving the Republic without permission. Mandela, the 44-year-old former lieutenant of Chief Albert Lutuli, leader of the African National Congress, turned the hearing into a political trial. The accused became the accuser. Owing to the Sabotage Act in South Africa his passionate defence was virtually unreported. These extracts are from his main addresses to the court.

MICHAEL PETO

NELSON MANDELA "driven to speak for what we believe is right . . ."

IN the course of this application I am frequently going to refer to the white man and to white people. I want at once to make it clear that I am not a racialist and do not support racialism of any kind, because to me racialism is a barbaric thing whether it comes from a black man or from a white man.

I challenge the right of this Court to hear my case on two grounds:—

Firstly, I challenge it on the ground that I will not be given a fair and proper trial.

Secondly, I consider myself neither morally nor legally obliged to obey laws made by a Parliament in which I am not represented.

In a political trial such as the present one, which involves a clash of the aspirations of the African people and those of whites, the country's Courts, as presently constituted, cannot be impartial and fair. In such cases, whites are interested parties. A judiciary controlled entirely by whites and enforcing laws enacted by a white Parliament in which we have no representation—laws which in most cases are passed in the face of unanimous opposition from Africans—cannot be regarded as an impartial tribunal in a political trial where an African stands as an accused.

Surface rights

It is true that an African who is charged in a Court of Law enjoys on the surface the same rights and privileges as a white accused in so far as the conduct of his trial is concerned. He is governed by the same rules of procedure and evidence as apply to a white accused. But it would be grossly inaccurate to conclude from this fact that an African consequently enjoys equality before the law.

In its proper meaning equality before the law means the right to participate in the making of the laws by which one is governed, a Constitution which guarantees democratic rights to all sections of the population, the right to approach the Court for protection or relief for the violation of rights guaranteed in the Constitution, and the right to take part in the administration of justice as judges, magistrates, attorneys-general, law advisers and similar positions.

The white man makes all the laws, he charges us before his Courts and accuses us, and he sits in judgment over us. The real purpose of this rigid colour bar is to ensure that the justice dispensed by the Courts should conform to the policy of the country, however much that policy might be in conflict with the norms of justice accepted in judiciaries throughout the civilised world.

The existence of genuine democratic values amongst some of the country's whites in the judiciary, however slender they may be, is welcomed by me. I hate racial discrimination most intensely and in all its manifestations. I have fought it all along my life. I fight it now, and will do so until the end of my days. Even although I now happen to be tried by one whose opinion I hold in high esteem, I detest most violently the set-up that surrounds me here. It makes me feel that I am a black man in a white man's Court. This should not be. I should feel perfectly free, at ease and at home with the assurance that I am being tried by a fellow South African who does not regard me as inferior, entitled to a special type of justice.

We regard the struggle against colour discrimination and for the pursuit of freedom and happiness as the highest aspiration of all men. Through bitter experience, we have learnt to regard the white man as a harsh and merciless type of human being whose contempt for our rights, and whose utter indifference to the promotion of our welfare, makes his assurances to us absolutely meaningless and hypocritical.

In order that the Court shall understand the frame of mind which leads me to action such as this [to call for a national strike on the day South Africa became a Republic], it is necessary for me to explain the background to my own political development and to try to make this Court aware of the factors that influenced me in deciding to act as I did.

Many years ago, when I was a boy brought up in my village in the Transkei, I listened to the elders of the tribe telling stories about the good old days, before the arrival of the white man. I hoped and vowed then that, among the treasures that life might offer me, would be the opportunity to serve my people and make my own humble contribution to their freedom struggles.

Unity of all

When I reached adult stature, I became a member of the African National Congress. That was in 1944, and I have followed its policy, supported it and believed in its aims and outlook for 18 years. Its policy was one which appealed to my deepest inner convictions. It sought for the unity of all Africans, overriding tribal differences amongst them. It sought the acquisition of political power for Africans in the land of their birth. The African National Congress further believed that all people, irrespective of the national groups to which they may belong, and irrespective of the colour of their skins, all people whose home is South Africa and who believe in the principles of democracy and of equality of men, should be treated as Africans; that all South Africans are entitled to live a free life on the basis of fullest equality of the rights and opportunities in every field, of full democratic rights, with a direct say in the affairs of the Government.

Right at the beginning of my career as an attorney I encountered difficulties imposed on me because of the colour of my skin and further difficulty surrounding me because of my membership and support of the African National Congress. In the Courts where we practised we were constantly aware that no matter how well, how correctly, how adequately we pursued our career of law, we could not become a prosecutor, or a magistrate or a judge. We became aware of the fact that as attorneys we often dealt with officials whose competence and attainments were no higher than ours, but whose superior position was maintained and protected by a white skin.

Upholding dignity

I regarded it as a duty which I owed, not just to my people, but also to my profession, to cry out against this discrimination which is essentially unjust and opposed to the whole basis of the attitude towards justice which is part of the tradition of legal training in this country. I believed that in taking up a stand against this injustice I was upholding the dignity of what should be an honourable profession.

Your Warship, I would say that the whole life of any thinking African in this country drives him continuously to a conflict peculiar to this country. The law as it is applied, the law as it has been developed over a long period of history, and especially the law as it is written and designed by the Nationalist Government, is a law which, in our view, is *immoral, unjust and intolerable.* Our consciences dictate that we must protest against it, that we must oppose it and that we must attempt to alter it.

Always we have been conscious of our obligations as citizens to avoid breaches of the law, where such breaches can be avoided, to prevent clash between the authorities and our people where such clash can be prevented, but nevertheless we have been driven to speak up for what we believe is right, and work for it and try to bring about changes which will satisfy our human conscience.

If I had my time over I would do the same again, so would any man who dares call himself a man.

We have been conditioned to our attitudes by history which is not of our making. We have been conditioned by the history of white Government in this country to accept the fact that Africans, when they make their demands strongly and powerfully enough for those demands to have some chance of success, will be met by force and terror on the part of the Government. This is not something we have taught the African people, this is something the African people have learned from their own bitter experience.

Government violence can do only one thing and that is to breed counter-violence. We have warned repeatedly that the Government, by resorting continually to violence, will breed, in this country, counter-violence amongst the people, till ultimately, if there is no dawning of sanity on the part of the Government, ultimately the dispute between the Government and my people will finish up by being settled in violence and by force. Already there are indications in this country that people, my people, Africans, are turning to deliberate acts of violence and of force against the Government, in order to persuade the Government, in the only language which this Government shows, by its own behaviour, that it understands.

Striving for good

Elsewhere in the world, a Court would say to me, "You should have made representations to the Government." This Court, I am confident, will not say so. Representations have been made, by people who have gone before me, time and time again.

Nor will the Court, I believe, say that, under the circumstances, my people are condemned for ever to say nothing and to do nothing. If the Court says that, or believes it, I think it is mistaken and deceiving itself. Men are not capable of doing nothing, of saying nothing, of not reacting to injustice, of not protesting against oppression, of not striving for the good society and the good life in the ways they see it. Nor will they do so in this country.

Perhaps the Court will say that despite our human rights to protest, to object, to make ourselves heard, we should stay within the letter of the law. I would say, sir, that it is the Government, its administration of the law, which brings the law into such contempt and disrepute that one is no longer concerned in this country to stay within the letter of the law. I will illustrate this from my own experience. The Government has used the process of law to handicap me, in my personal life, in my career and in my political work in a way which is calculated, in my opinion, to bring a contempt for the law.

I found myself trailed by officers of the Security Branch of the police force wherever I went. In short I found myself treated as a criminal, an unconvicted criminal. I was not allowed to pick my company, to frequent the company of men, to participate in their political activities, to join their organisations. I was not free from constant police surveillance any more than a convict in one of our gaols is free from surveillance. I was made, by the law, a criminal, not because of what I had done, but of what I stood for, because of what I thought, because of my conscience. Can it be any wonder to anybody that such conditions make a man an outlaw of society? Can it be wondered that such a man, having been outlawed by the Government, should be prepared to lead the life of an outlaw, as I have led for some months, according to the evidence before this Court?

Separation

It has not been easy for me during the past period to separate myself from my wife and children, to say goodbye to the good old days when, at the end of a strenuous day at an office, I could look forward to joining my family at the dinner-table, and instead to take up the life of a man hunted continuously by the police, living separated from those who are closest to me, in my own country, facing continually the hazards of detection and of arrest. This has been a life infinitely more difficult than serving a prison sentence. No man in his right senses would voluntarily choose such a life in preference to the one of normal, family, social life which exists in every civilised community.

Police persecution

But there comes a time, as it came in my life, when a man is denied the right to live a normal life, when he can live only the life of an outlaw because the Government has so decreed to use the law to impose a state of outlawry upon him. I was driven to this situation and I do not regret having taken the decisions that I did take. Other people will be driven in the same way in this country, by this same very force of police persecution and of administrative action by the Government, to follow my course, of that I am certain.

I must place on record my belief that I have been only one in a large army of people, to all of whom the credit for any success of achievement is due. Advance and progress is not the result of my work alone, but of the collective work of my colleagues and I, both here and abroad.

I do not believe, Your Worship, that this Court, in inflicting penalties, will deter men from the course that they believe is right. History shows that penalties do not deter men when their conscience is aroused, nor will they deter my people or the colleagues with whom I have worked before.

I am prepared to pay the penalty even though I know how bitter and desperate is the situation of an African in the prisons of this country. I have been in these prisons and I know how gross is the discrimination, even behind the prison walls, against Africans, how much worse is the condition of the treatment meted out to African prisoners than that accorded to whites. More powerful than my fear of the dreadful conditions to which I might be subjected in prison is my hatred for the dreadful conditions to which my people are subjected outside prison throughout this country.

Racial arrogance

I hate the practice of race discrimination, and in doing so, in my hatred, I am sustained by the fact that the overwhelming majority of mankind hates it equally. I hate the systematic inculcation of children with colour prejudice and I am sustained in that hatred by the fact that the overwhelming majority of mankind, here and abroad, are with me in that. I hate the racial arrogance which decrees that the good things of life shall be retained as the exclusive right of a minority of the population, and which reduces the majority of the population to a subservience and inferiority, and maintains them as voteless chattels to work where they are told and behave as they are told by the ruling minority.

Nothing that this Court can do to me will change in any way that hatred in me, which can only be removed by the removal of the injustice and the inhumanity which I have sought to remove from the political, social and economic life of this country.

Whatever sentence Your Worship sees fit to impose upon me for the crime for which I have been convicted before this Court, may it rest assured that when my sentence has been completed I will still be moved, as men are always moved, by their consciences. I will still be moved to dislike of the race discrimination against my people when I come out from serving my sentence, to take up again, as best I can, the struggle for the removal of those injustices until they are finally abolished once and for all.

Nelson Mandela's defence reported in full in the London Observer.

want to perform work which they are capable of doing and not work which the government declares them to be capable of. Africans want to be allowed to live where they obtain work and not endorsed out of an area because they were not born there. Africans want to be allowed to own land in places where they work and not be obliged to live in rented houses which they can never call their own. Africans want to be part of the general population and not confined to living in their own ghettoes. African men want to have their wives and children to live with them where they work and not be forced into an unnatural existence in men's hostels. African women want to be with their men folk and not be left permanently widowed in the reserves. Africans want to be allowed out after eleven o'clock at night and not be confined to their rooms like little children. Africans want to be allowed to travel in their own country and to seek work where they want to and not where the labour bureau tells them to. Africans want a just share in the whole of South Africa; they want security and a stake in society.

Above all, we want equal political rights, because without them our disabilities will be permanent.

Nelson Mandela, together with six of the other defendants, was sentenced to life imprisonment on Robben Island.

The government continued to strengthen the apparatus of oppression, and organized African political activities were virtually wiped out inside South Africa. In 1969 a new organization, the Bureau of State Security, commonly known as "BOSS", was created to take charge of all matters relating to state security. But protest continued in non-political forms. Students and church people staged protests, sometimes jointly, as in demonstrations in 1972 at the Anglican Cathedrals in Cape Town and Johannesburg. In the early 1970s there was an upsurge of trade union activity. It was not illegal for Africans to form unions, but these had no legal recognition and strikes were illegal. In 1973 strikes on a large scale broke out in and around Durban. For once the government thought it prudent to handle the situation gently.

Steve Biko

It was among students that the Black Consciousness Movement began, and in 1972 the Black Peoples' Convention was set up to provide a political platform for Africans. The movement, like the banned PAC, believed that Africans would not achieve anything until they had won the psychological struggle to restore confidence in themselves. Unlike the PAC, the new movement was open to all oppressed and voteless people, but rejected anyone who was a collaborator with the apartheid system. This included the leaders of the "Bantustans". The outstanding leader of the movement was Steve Biko. He was

A serious wave of strikes by black workers broke out in 1973 especially around Durban.

essentially against violence and anxious for a moderate solution through dialogue and negotiation. In 1977 he was nevertheless arrested. He died later the same year, as had an increasing number of other detainees, from treatment received while in police custody. The Minister of Justice, Mr James Kruger, made matters worse by his insensitive comments on Biko's death. Public opinion, both inside and outside South Africa, forced the government to hold an enquiry during which it was established that his death had been the result of police brutality.

Soweto 1976

Most important of all the African protests in recent years was the great explosion of anger and discontent which began in Soweto but spread to several other areas in June 1976. Soweto is the

name of a group of black townships some thirty miles southwest of Johannesburg. It is the biggest concentration of Africans anywhere in the country. Its population is predominantly young. Over half its people are under twenty. On paper, the facilities of Soweto seem good by African standards. But for those who work in Johannesburg life is an unending treadmill. They leave home early in the morning and return late at night after a twice-daily struggle on crowded commuter trains. The protest began among secondary school pupils who boycotted exams in revolt against regulations that require some of their instruction to be given in Afrikaans. It developed into a massive challenge to the system of apartheid.

There was never any danger that the authorities would lose control or that the government would fall. But they were forced, reluctantly, with the world looking on and listening in, to make use of the overwhelming apparatus of force which keeps them in power. The events in Soweto and other cities in June and July 1976 made the Sharpeville incident seem trivial. The difference in the scale of the protests was significant. It is hardly possible to accept the government's explanation that they were all the result of agitators. The security system is too

The wife and son of Steve Biko at the Black Consciousness leader's funeral in 1977.

Whites as well as blacks demonstrated against apartheid. White students demonstrate in Johannesburg.

Soweto disturbances, June 1976. Some grievances of the people of Soweto: a crowded commuter train (above); and school children protest against having classes in Afrikaans (below).

Rioters in Soweto use cars as road blocks.

efficient for that to be so. The report of Mr Justice Cillie who conducted the government's own enquiry into the causes of the Soweto disturbances dismissed the idea that they were the result of the work of communist agitators and placed the blame on the country's racial policies. What happened was the almost inevitable result of the frustration and resentment of a new generation of Africans. They are more aware of the nature of the system that exploits them. They are also aware of the extent of the outside world's disapproval of that system and of the increasing pressure which that disapproval exerts on the South African government and people. It is time to look at the relations between South Africa and the outside world since 1948.

Massive force finally quelled the riots.

SOUTH AFRICA, APARTHEID AND THE REST OF THE WORLD

South Africa's leaders have often complained that the rest of the world does not understand the country's racial problems. South Africa's problems, they say, are unique. People who do not live in South Africa are in no position to criticize apartheid. Mr Vorster, when Prime Minister, made this point in 1970:

> Each country must solve its own problems in its own way for it is only when one lives in a country and comes into daily contact with all aspects of life that a true assessment of the situation can be made and policies formulated accordingly.

Another explanation offered by South African leaders in reply to the almost universal criticism of their race policies, is that South Africa found herself caught up in the rivalry between the United States and the Soviet Union in their bid for the support of the African and Asian countries and of the Third World in general. Speaking in Parliament about the critical attitude of the United Nations in 1961, Dr Verwoerd said:

> Both the Western Bloc and the Communist Bloc seek the support of the Afro-Asian Bloc. South Africa is landed in the position where both sides attack her because in this way the friendship of the Afro-Asian countries can be sought.

There is some truth in both of these views, but they are important for what they reveal about South Africa's response to criticism of her policies. South Africans do not want to believe that their race policies are as bad as the world makes out. Therefore, they cast around for reasons to discredit the criticisms or to attack the motives of the critics. A further tactic adopted increasingly in the 1960s was to counter-attack and point to the violation of human rights in those countries, many of them in Africa, which led the attacks on South Africa.

Outside South Africa there are those who argue that criticism is counter-productive and will merely strengthen South Africa's resolve to enforce her policies. There is some evidence for this. But it is equally certain that to keep silent would be still less likely to produce any change of heart. There is little doubt that many South Africans miss the sporting fixtures at international level, such as cricket and rugby union matches, which have been stopped as a result of bans imposed by Commonwealth countries. So far, these bans have merely produced limited and deceptive reforms in an attempt to have sporting contacts restored. A continuation of the bans may produce more genuine moves towards multi-racialism in South African sport.

At the more serious level of diplomacy and international trade, there can be no doubt that the South African government has long been worried by the growing criticism and the increasing danger of isolation and boycott by the international community. International criticism of South Africa began soon after the Second World War and was a part of the new attitude to racial questions that became general at the time. A foretaste of what was to come was experienced in the very first session of the General Assembly of the United Nations in 1946, when India was critical of recent legislation which had damaged the interests of Asians in South Africa. The criticism mounted as, one after the other, the colonial territories in Africa and Asia attained their independence and became members of the international community.

The possible consequences of the United Nations resolutions became more serious in 1960. Until that date the resolutions were merely verbal condemnations. South Africa's attempts to put a stop to them, by claiming that they constituted interference in her internal affairs, were not accepted. Her policies, the critics replied, were violations of human rights and a matter of international concern. After 1960 resolutions began to claim that South Africa's policies were a threat to international peace and resolutions were then often accompanied by calls for action, usually in the field of trade. In 1964 the General Assembly of the UN called for a ban on the export of arms to South Africa, which both the United States and Britain supported. The number of countries who opposed or abstained from voting against such resolutions fell away almost completely. At an African level, the Organization of African Unity (OAU) called upon all its members in 1963 to close their air space to South African aircraft.

All South Africa's attempts to defend or justify herself were unacceptable. She argued that, after 1959 and the Promotion of. Bantu Self-Government Act, she was involved in the same kind of decolonizing process as countries like Britain and France. On the contrary, her opponents argued, she was one of the last relics of white colonialism on the continent. The only compensation for South Africa for the embarrassing and wearing sessions at the United Nations was that they tended to unite white South Africans more solidly behind the Nationalist government. This showed in succeeding elections. Moreover, South Africa valued her continued membership of the UN since it did at least provide her with a platform where she could try to defend herself. Her growing isolation was evident in other ways. Visits from ships of the United States fleet were called off; so were visits from cricket and rugby teams, ballet companies, theatre companies and other cultural organizations.

However, by the middle of the 1960s there were signs that on the international scene things were beginning to get better. It began, as the more positive approach to apartheid had begun, under Dr Verwoerd. Though there were ups and downs, the improvement lasted for nearly ten years. In the first place, both South Africa and her critics realized that trade embargoes were unlikely to be universally accepted and, even if they were, they would be of little effect because South Africa was nearer to being self-sufficient than most other countries. South Africa's main trading partners, like the USA, Britain and France, had actually expanded their trade with her. One African country, Kenya, complained that her withdrawal of trade had merely benefitted other countries who had eagerly taken her place. South Africa's economy was booming again after a temporary set-back following Sharpeville, and foreign investment was high.

Relations with Black Africa

Dr Verwoerd, after flirting with the idea of trying to attract the British High Commission Territories, assured them and the world in 1964 that he had abandoned all his claims to them. "We want to have the best possible relations for the sake of our common safety and economic interests". He went on to refer to a group of African countries that were prepared to cooperate economically. The promotion of South Africa's economic interests was central to the whole period of détente which followed. While trying to put over a new image of a country moving away from racial discrimination to a policy of separate development through the "Bantustans", South Africa was busy investing in and trading with the countries to the north. These "feelers" for economic links with black Africa were put out against the background of a new flourishing of the South African economy and the failure of independent Africa, by contrast, to achieve any economic progress or political stability. South Africa was relieved when the High Commission Territories each became independent under a moderate and, in all cases, largely traditional government. Shortly before his assassination in 1966, Dr Verwoerd had a meeting in Pretoria with Chief Jonathan, the Lesotho (Basutoland) Prime Minister.

The détente with Africa gathered momentum under Mr Balthazar Johannes (John) Vorster, who succeeded Dr Verwoerd as Prime Minister. He was ably supported by his Foreign Minister, the much travelled and very experienced Dr Muller, who had already served two years under Dr Verwoerd. Mr Vorster said that he wanted to participate with the international community, but that it must be understood that there was no question of South Africa giving up her policy of separate development as the price of international acceptance. As for Africa, Mr Vorster said: "The Republic is inspired by only one desire as regards the rest of Africa. It is to live in peace and friendship with the non-white states." At the beginning of 1967 Chief Jonathan of Lesotho flew to Cape Town in a South African airforce plane to begin a state visit. Within the next two years South Africa established good relations with Botswana and Swaziland.

Détente with Black Africa. Dr Verwoerd receives Chief Jonathan, Prime Minister of Lesotho, in Pretoria in 1966.

Further afield also there had been successes for the policy of détente. When Malawi became independent, Dr Banda, the President, dissociated his country from the general attitude of the OAU. His country's economic ties with South Africa were close and included the annual engagement of many thousands of migrant workers in the South African mines. To sever such links would have cost Malawi dearly. In 1966 Dr Banda signed a trade agreement with South Africa. In 1968 Malawi became the first black African country to establish a diplomatic mission in Cape Town. Three years later this became a full embassy, and Malawi's first ambassador was black. Mr Vorster made an official visit to Malawi in 1970. Later that year a further opening seemed to be offered when President Felix Houphouet-Boigny of the Ivory Coast said that he was in favour of dialogue with South Africa. His initiative was welcomed by a few African heads of state, mainly in French-speaking Africa, but was condemned by others.

The outlook was still not too bleak, even when the fall of the Caetano regime in Portugal led to Portugal's sudden abandonment of her African territories. In Angola and Mozambique African nationalist movements had already fought a long and increasingly successful struggle for independence and now Portugal's will to resist any longer crumbled. Mozambique was even more closely dependent than Malawi on her economic links with South Africa. The new Marxist regime there could not afford any dramatic gestures against South Africa for some time at least. In 1974 Vorster, buoyed up by an increasing majority as the result of an election, spoke of his willingness to aid other African countries in their development. Dr Kenneth Kaunda, President of Zambia, welcomed this announcement as "the voice of reason for which Africa and the rest of the world had been waiting". He was aware of the key role that South Africa could play in bringing about a settlement in the problem of Rhodesia which had been cut off from the international community since the white government of the country made its unilateral declaration of independence (UDI) in 1965. Rhodesia had then been subjected to a trade ban imposed by the United Nations and this had been specially harmful to Zambia whose main trading outlets to the sea had been through Rhodesia. Vorster visited the Ivory Coast later in 1974 and Liberia early in 1975. The climax and the highest hopes for the policy of détente came with the meeting of Mr Vorster and Dr Kaunda in a railway coach on the Victoria Falls Bridge in August 1975. They met in an attempt to find a solution to the ten-year-old Rhodesia crisis. Both stood to benefit if they were successful. The South African government had begun to bring pressure to bear on the Rhodesian government to reach a compromise that would satisfy African opinion. The attempt failed.

Before the end of the year the policy of détente was in ruins and the international position of South Africa had changed dramatically for the worse. This was the result of South Africa's ill-advised decision to intervene in the Angolan civil war in 1975. The circumstances of this intervention are still not clear. It is probable that South Africa's action was secretly encouraged by the USA, France and several African countries including Zaire, Zambia and the Ivory Coast. The object was to try to ensure the victory of the pro-Western UNITA forces and to defeat the Russian-backed, Marxist MPLA. South African intervention was countered by Cuban intervention and large supplies of Russian equipment. The South Africans decided that to continue the intervention was too risky and withdrew their forces.

The results were disastrous for South Africa. Her intervention was condemned as aggression by a UN resolution, while Cuba escaped censure. African opinion, previously split evenly between the two rival Angolan forces, lined up behind the MPLA which was installed with Cuban backing. Black Africa was solidly united against South Africa. To make matters worse this setback in the international field was soon followed in June 1976 by the events in Soweto (page 54). Vorster resigned the premiership in 1978, apparently for health reasons, and was soon installed as state President. Not long afterwards came the first revelations in the South African press of what came to be known as the "Muldergate Scandal". It was closely linked with South Africa's international position, because it arose from the activities of a special operation mounted by the

Détente with Black Africa. Mr Vorster meets President Kaunda of Zambia in a railway carriage on the Victoria Falls Bridge in August 1975. This attempt to solve the Rhodesian crisis ended in failure.

Ministry of Information to try to improve South Africa's image abroad. It was alleged that government funds had been misused by officials involved and that this had been done with the knowledge of government ministers. Connie Mulder, the Minister of Information, was the first to be forced to resign and later Mr Vorster resigned the Presidency. South Africans who had supposed that Afrikaner politicians were honest and not given to corrupt practices were shaken by the long-drawn-out affair. In the face of this succession of setbacks at home and abroad and the resulting pressures, the question was inevitably asked: Will the South African government feel so threatened and isolated that it will be unable to resist demands for modifications to its policy of apartheid?

THE POSSIBILITIES OF CHANGE

To try to answer the question posed at the end of the last chapter is to move from history into prophecy. South Africa's racial policies, whether they have gone under the name of "segregation" or "apartheid", have never been static. While the end has remained constant — the maintenance of political and economic domination and control by the white minority — the means have been changed and modified to meet changing circumstances.

In the 1940s, during the rapid expansion of South Africa's manufacturing industries, many industrialists and others began to argue that the migrant labour system, which was an essential feature of the segregation policies, could not provide the skilled and semi-skilled labour force required to enable the new industries to flourish. The time had come to recognize the existence of a permanent and therefore stable African labour force in the white towns. This could entail the recognition of some form of political rights for such Africans. Smuts and his United Party seemed, after the Second World War, to be on the brink of accepting this view. Dr Malan and the newly emerging National Party were totally opposed to any such policy. White workers, fearing for their jobs, voted for the Nationalists in the 1948 election. The industrialists were apprehensive and feared that the whole labour force might become migrant and therefore unstable. In fact, it soon became clear that apartheid provided an answer to their problem without sacrificing any of the fundamental features of white racial policy. The adoption of the idea of "homelands" and the insistence that all urban Africans would hold full citizenship only in the homelands, created a class of "permanent-temporary" workers in the white urban areas.

More recently, arguments similar to those heard in the late 1940s have been advanced, predicting that apartheid will be undermined by the needs of an advancing economy. There is no reason to suppose, however, that the system will be any less adaptable than it was then. South African racial policy has always been closely geared to the needs of the economy and it has served those needs very effectively. An ailing and declining economy is more likely to undermine and threaten apartheid than a healthy and expanding one. The remarkable rise in the world price of gold in 1979 and early 1980 will have helped to improve apartheid's chances of survival.

It has always been rash in South Africa to read too much into statements or reports which seem to herald changes in the system. They often lead to little change or indeed to a worsening of the position of Africans and other non-whites. The last thirty years are littered with a trail of false hopes. After Sharpeville in 1960 the Deputy Prime Minister told the world that the "old book of South African history was closed". In 1974 Johannesburg City Council took steps to eliminate "petty apartheid", and its example was followed in other major cities like Durban, Cape Town and Pietermaritzburg: but these were the trimmings of the system and were expendable. In 1975 the Prime Minister, Mr Vorster, and the Foreign Minister, Pik Botha, speaking at the United Nations, both seemed to hold out a promise of major changes. No changes took place, perhaps because of the worsening international position of the country. In 1978 the government gave certain Africans, already holding the right to "permanent" residence in urban areas, the right to own leasehold property in the townships. In reality, they were merely restoring rights which had been abolished in 1967 and which themselves were a diminution of the rights held by some Africans in Sophiatown and elsewhere before the Group Areas Act of 1950.

Perhaps there was more reason to believe that the fundamentals of apartheid were about to be

Relaxation of "petty" apartheid. These benches in a pleasant square in the centre of Johannesburg are no longer reserved for the use of whites or non-whites.

changed when, in 1979, the Wiehahn and the Riekert Commissions issued reports. The Wiehahn Commission was concerned with Africans' trade union rights and the Riekert Commission with the pass laws and Influx Control. These reports, therefore, certainly touched the important areas of economic power and control. At a superficial look, they seemed to promise significant concessions to Africans in these two vital areas. White trade union leaders were alarmed; some Africans gave the reports a cautious welcome. However, closer study of what had been recommended suggested that something much more subtle and much more in line with traditional white policy was being proposed. If the reports were implemented, only a limited number of Africans, again those with permanent residential rights in the townships, would be affected. The remainder, the great majority of urban Africans, would probably be more strictly controlled than ever. It is possible that the recommendations could lead to a closer scrutiny of Africans living

in urban areas; and this, in turn, could lead to the expulsion of large numbers of Africans to the already overcrowded Bantustans. The final result would be a tightening, rather than a relaxation, of control.

It has been suggested that the Commissions' recommendations may be part of a government strategy to win the support of an elite of urban Africans by offering them a better economic and social future; and that this strategy is a response to the growing pressures against apartheid from both inside and outside South Africa. Such a deal, with a minority of urban Africans, is likely to succeed only if the government's broader policy of creating Bantustans wins much wider acceptance than it has achieved so far. In fact, this policy, the ideological core of apartheid, has failed. There is no recognition of the policy outside the white establishment in South Africa. No foreign country has recognized the Bantustans that have so far been granted "independence". The leaders of the Bantustans have continued to press for additional territory. A growing movement among Africans, with some support and encouragement from whites, to reject independence both on the grounds that it is not genuine independence and also that it implies acceptance of the system poses a greater threat. Chief Buthelezi, the leader of Kwazulu, made his opposition clear at an early stage. At the head of his "Inkatha" movement, he represents a powerful African political force in South Africa. The movement, which was originally reserved for the people of Kwazulu, opened its ranks to other Africans in 1979 and Buthelezi has campaigned for support in Soweto. Early in 1980 a mixed commission of experts from South Africa and overseas advised the Ciskei, one of the two Xhosa homelands, against accepting independence and recommended as an alternative a link with a neighbouring white area to form a multi-racial region. This course of action is unlikely to be accepted by the South African government, even though the President of the Afrikaner Chamber of Commerce and several Afrikaner academics were among those who made the recommendation.

This should be no surprise. As this history has shown, Afrikaners have often been divided among themselves. At the present time, at the beginning of the 1980s, they are once again divided while the debate about how South Africa should face its growing crisis continues. The hardliners on the right have already dissociated themselves from the main body of Afrikaner Nationalists and have established a new party, the Herstigte Nasionale Party (HNP), led by Albert Hertzog, son of the former Prime Minister. The Afrikaners as a whole are divided into the "Verligtes" (the enlightened ones) and the "Verkramptes" (the narrowminded ones). Mr Vorster and Mr Pieter Botha, who followed him as Prime Minister in 1978, both belonged to the former group. Some of Mr Pieter Botha's statements have shocked not only the Verkramptes but many of the middle-

Mr Pieter Botha visiting Soweto in 1979, the first Prime Minister to do so. He has increasingly suggested reforms in racial policies and there has been much speculation about how far he is prepared to go.

of-the-road Afrikaners as well. In 1979, for example, he hinted at the possibility of amending laws as basic as the Mixed Marriages Act and the Immorality Amendment Act. At four by-elections fought in the Transvaal heartland of the National Party in October 1979 there were signs that such hints were losing the party much of its traditional support. The National Party candidates all won, but by a much reduced majority; and the HNP candidates were the only ones who could draw any comfort from the results.

As yet, this withdrawal of support for the National Party does not seem to have frightened the Prime Minister into abandoning his talk of change. It is possible that the strategy of a deal with an African urban elite has a place in his thinking and that the National Party hopes to compensate for the loss of its right-wing sup-porters by attracting the support of even more English-speaking South Africans. It is worth remembering, however, that in all the talk of possible change in recent years, nothing has been said by Mr Botha, or by any other white politi-cian with the remotest chance of holding power, about sharing political power with Africans — not even with an African elite. It is impossible to envisage any African leader with a significant following being satisfied with anything less than power sharing.

At the time of writing (March 1980), the long-drawn-out Rhodesian crisis appears to be approaching a democratic solution. White Rhodesians have been driven to accept this by several years of bloody war, which they finally realized they could not win. Will white South Africans have to go through the same painful and violent process before they, in turn, accept the need for a similar solution?

DATE LIST

The main segregation and apartheid laws are in CAPITAL LETTERS. Events outside South Africa with an impact on South Africa appear in *italics*.

AD

4th century The first Bantu-speakers move south across Limpopo river.

8th century Bantu-speakers building in stone on Highveld in the Transvaal.

c.1000 Widespread Iron Age settlements of Bantu-speakers in the Transvaal.

1000-1800 Bantu-speakers continue to spread southwards.

1487 Bartholomew Diaz rounds the Cape.

1497 Vasco da Gama sails up the East African coast.

1652 First Dutch settlers at the Cape.

1688 French Huguenots arrive at the Cape.

18th century Increasing contacts between Boer (Dutch) farmers and Xhosa (Bantu-speakers) in region of Gamtoos and Great Fish rivers.

1779 First Xhosa War (nine in all between 1779 and 1878).

1789 *Beginning of the French Revolution.*

1794 *French occupy Holland.*

1795 First British occupation of the Cape.

1802 Cape returned to Dutch.

1806 Second British occupation of the Cape.

1807 *British abolish the Slave Trade.*

1812 Black Circuit Court.

1815 Britain retains the Cape at end of Napoleonic Wars.

1819 Dr John Philip arrives at the Cape.

1820 5000 British settlers arrive at Port Elizabeth.

c.1818-30 Mfecane: wars between Bantu-speaking peoples of southern Africa.

1836 The Great Trek begins.

1838 Battle of Blood River: Trekkers defeat Zulu leader, Dingaan.

1843 British annex Natal: many Boers trek again.

1852 Independent Boer Republic in Transvaal.

1854 Independent Boer Republic in Orange Free State.

1858 and 1865 Basuto Wars between Boers and Moshesh, leader of Basuto.

1860 Indian labour imported for sugar plantations in Natal.

1867 Discovery of diamonds near borders of Orange Free State.

1868 British protectorate in Basutoland.

1872 Cape Province granted Responsible Government.

1877 Britain annexes the Transvaal.

1879 Zulu War between Britain and Zulus.

1880 First Boer War, British against Boers: British defeated.

1881 and 1884 Pretoria and London Conventions: limited independence of Transvaal (South African Republic).

1882 Paul Kruger becomes President of South African Republic.

1886 Discovery of gold on the Witwatersrand in the Transvaal.

1889 *British South Africa Company granted a Royal Charter with administrative rights in Rhodesia.*

1890 Rhodes becomes Prime Minister of Cape Province. British South Africa Company begins to exploit Rhodesia.

1895 Jameson Raid by British South Africa troops into the Transvaal.

1899-1902 Second Boer War between British and Boers of Transvaal and Orange Free state.

1902 Peace of Vereeniging.

1910 Union of South Africa established. Botha first Prime Minister.

1911 MINES AND WORKS ACT: COLOUR

BAR IN INDUSTRY.

1912 African National Congress founded.
Afrikaner Nationalist Party founded by Hertzog.

1913 NATIVES LAND ACT: DEFINES AFRICAN RESERVES.

1914 *First World War begins: South Africa fights on side of Britain.*

1915 South African troops overrun German South West Africa.

1919 South Africa given mandate over South West Africa.
Smuts becomes Prime Minister on death of Botha.

1922 Rand Revolt staged by white miners on the Rand.

1923 NATIVE URBAN AREAS ACT: REGULATES NON-WHITES IN TOWNS.

1924 African Nationalists and Labour Party defeat Smuts: Hertzog Prime Minister at head of "Pact" Government.

1925 Afrikaans replaces Dutch as one of two official languages in South Africa.

1926 MINES AND WORKS ACT: TIGHTENS INDUSTRIAL COLOUR BAR.

1931 *Statute of Westminster confirms sovereignty of the Dominions within the British Commonwealth.*

1934 "Fusion" of Hertzog's Nationalist Party and Smuts' South Africa Party to form the United Party.

1936 HERTZOG'S SEGREGATION LAWS: AFRICANS LOSE THE VOTE IN THE CAPE.

1938 Centenary celebrations of Battle of Blood River.

1939 Hertzog defeated on "Neutrality" vote: Smuts becomes Prime Minister.
Second World War begins.

1945 *United Nations Charter.*

1946 *United Nations refuses South Africa's request to incorporate South West Africa.*

1947 *India becomes independent.*

1948 Dr Malan and the National Party win the general election.
"Apartheid" becomes new name for government's racial policy.

1949 PROHIBITION OF MIXED MARRIAGES ACT.

1950 IMMORALITY AMENDMENT ACT: POPULATION REGISTRATION ACT: SUPPRESSION OF COMMUNISM ACT:
Death of Smuts.

1951 BANTU AUTHORITIES ACT.

1952 ANC organizes Defiance Campaign.
ABOLITION OF PASSES AND CO-ORDINATION OF DOCUMENTS ACT.

1953 BANTU EDUCATION ACT: RESERVATION OF SEPARATE AMENITIES ACT (PETTY APARTHEID).
Luthuli President of the ANC.

1954 Strijdom Prime Minister.

1955 Congress of the People draws up the Freedom Charter.

1956 CAPE COLOUREDS LOSE THE VOTE IN CAPE PROVINCE.
Treason Trial begins.

1957 *Ghana becomes independent (the first British colony to do so).*

1958 Dr Verwoerd Prime Minister.

1959 PROMOTION OF BANTU SELF-GOVERNMENT ACT; EXTENSION OF UNIVERSITY EDUCATION ACT.
Pan Africanist Congress formed under Robert Sobukwe.

1960 Sharpeville Shooting. ANC and PAC banned.

1960-64 *Most British and French Colonial territories become independent. Mounting criticism of South Africa's policies at United Nations.*

1961 Treason Trial ends. All acquitted. South Africa becomes a Republic and leaves the Commonwealth.

1961-64 GENERAL LAWS AMENDMENT ACTS: massive powers of repression taken by government including 90 days detention without trial.

1962 Nelson Mandela arrested: eventually sentenced to life imprisonment on Robben Island.

1963 Rivonia Trials begin.

1963 *Federation of Rhodesia and Nyasaland breaks up.*

1965 *Rhodesia declares unilateral independence (UDI).*

Guerilla war begins in Mozambique.

1965- South Africa attempts to promote
75   "détente" with Black Africa.

1966 Vorster Prime Minister.

1966 Guerilla activity begins in Rhodesia.

1969 GENERAL LAWS AMENDMENT ACT:
      "BOSS" set up.

1970 BANTU HOMELANDS CITIZENSHIP
      ACT: All Africans to become citizens
      of a "Homeland".

1971 BANTU HOMELANDS CONSTITUTION
      ACT: limited powers of self govern-
      ment to "Homelands".

1972 Black Consciousness Movement emerges:
      Black Peoples Convention formed.

1973 Serious wave of strikes amongst African
      workers.

*1974 Revolution in Portugal. Mozambique
      independent.*

*1975 Angola independent but Civil War follows.
      South Africa intervenes and then
      withdraws: end of "détente".*

1976 Transkei made "independent". Soweto
      disturbances begin and spread to other
      urban areas.

1978 Bophuthatswana "independent". Mr
      Pieter Botha becomes Prime Minister.
      Steve Biko, Black Consciousness leader
      dies in police custody. Internal settle-
      ment in Namibia fails to gain accept-
      ance.

1979 "Muldergate" scandal comes to a head.
      Internal settlement attempted in
      Rhodesia fails to gain acceptance.
      Wiehahn and Riekert Commissions
      report.

*1980 Lancaster House Conference prepares
      way for independence elections in
      Rhodesia (Zimbabwe). Zimbabwe inde-
      pendent under leadership of Mr Mugabe.*

      Mr Pieter Botha proposes a National
      Convention, including black leaders,
      to discuss South Africa's future.

GLOSSARY

As stated at the beginning of the book, the words describing the different groups of people in South Africa have different overtones and should be used with care.

The black peoples of South Africa

Africans This is the word which the black inhabitants themselves prefer and is free of the derogatory tone of most of the alternatives.

Bantu This word is commonly used by white South Africans in describing the black people and, until recently, was used in official government language. It is really a linguistic term and refers to the group of related languages spoken by most of South Africa's black people. In this book, therefore, the word "Bantu-speakers" is used. The Africans themselves do not like the word.

Natives This word is also often used by whites, especially English-speaking whites, for the black people in South Africa. It was the official term until "Bantu" replaced it. Illogically, it has been used to refer simply to blacks, regardless of whether they were born in the country or not. Africans resent the use of the word because of its derogatory tone.

Kaffirs This word has even more derogatory overtones and is therefore even more resented by Africans. It comes from an Arab word meaning "unbelievers" and was used by the Arabs on the East African coast. It was used especially by the frontier farmers to describe the first Bantu-speakers they encountered in large numbers, and it was carried to other parts of the country by the trekboers in the nineteenth century.

Khoikhoi This is the name which the people contemptuously called "Hottentots" by the early Dutch settlers use for themselves.

San The word used by the Khoikhoi to describe the most backward people of South Africa, whom the Dutch contemptuously called "Bushmen".

Khoisan This word is used by modern writers to describe collectively the Khoikhoi and the San.

The white peoples of South Africa

Whites Either this or *Europeans* is the usual word used. They are divided into two groups:

Afrikaners These people speak Afrikaans and are descendants of the early Dutch settlers. The language was developed mainly from Dutch but with a little French, Malay and English influence.

English-speakers These are the other main group of whites and include many comparatively recent immigrants.

The Coloureds

Cape Coloureds This term is used for people of mixed racial origin. In the early days they were mainly the product of interbreeding of Europeans and Malays or Khoikhoi, but the term has come to denote anyone of mixed breeding.

Indians Also called *Asians* or *Asiatics*. These are mostly the descendants of the indentured Indian labourers who came to work on the sugar plantations of Natal between 1860 and 1911.

Other terms

Non-Europeans Or *Non-whites.* These are widely used collective terms for all who are neither white nor European. They are resented because of their negative character.

Tribe This word is used to denote a group anywhere in Africa whose members have common cultural and social features and a common allegiance to a traditional authority. It has come to have overtones of inferiority and backwardness and is better avoided by using the neutral term *"people"*. The Bantu-speaking peoples of South Africa are divided into three main groups. These are the Nguni, who include the Xhosa, Zulu, Swazi, Tembu and Pondo; the Sotho, who include the North and South Sotho; and the Tswana.

Geographical terms

Reserves Land set aside for the exclusive use of Africans. This was done largely by the Natives Land Act of 1913 and the Native Trust and Land Act of 1936. After 1951 the reserves became the areas proposed as the *Bantu Homelands* or *Bantustans.*

Veld or *Veldt* Pasture or grassland. The *Highveld* at a height of 4000-6000 feet is on the plateau west of the Drakensberg mountains. The *Lowveld* lies between the Drakensberg escarpment and the Indian Ocean. Both areas were suitable for settlement and agricultural development by the Bantu-speakers and, later, by the white trekkers.

Witwatersrand or *Rand* The area, very rich in minerals, especially gold, which stretches east and west from Johannesburg. It is now the main centre for the other non-mining industries of South Africa.

BOOKS FOR FURTHER READING AND VISUAL AIDS

Gulley, P.R. and Hayward, K.E., *South Africa: Conflict and Co-operation* (Longman Paul, 1976)

Le May, G.H.L., *Black and White in South Africa: The Politics of Survival* (Macdonald Library of the 20th Century, 1971)

Marks, Shula, *South Africa: The myth of the Empty Land* (History Today, Volume 30, January 1980)

Marquand, L., *The Story of South Africa* (Faber, 1966 edition)

Sorrenson, K., *Separate and Unequal* (Heinemann, 1976)

Troup, Freda, *South Africa: An Historical Introduction* (Penguin, 1975)

Were, G., *A History of South Africa* (Evans, 1974)

Wilson, D., *A History of South and Central Africa* (C.U.P. 1975)

It is interesting to compare the material produced by organizations such as the Anti-Apartheid Movement and the International Defence and Aid Fund with material issued by the South African Embassy. A few examples are:

Rogers, Barbara, *Divide and Rule: South Africa's Bantustans* (IDAF, 1976)

Troup, Freda, *Forbidden Pastures: Education under Apartheid* (IDAF, 1976)

Compare the above with:

South Africa: Intergroup and Race Relations, 1970-77 — a Political Backgrounder (Issued by the Director of Information, South Africa House, London)

Stepping into the Future: Education for South Africa's Black, Coloured and Indian Peoples (Erudita Publications Ltd, Johannesburg, 1975)

An African view of apartheid can be seen in books like the following:

Desmond, C., *The Discarded People* (Penguin, 1970)

Luthuli, A., *Let My People Go* (Fontana, 1963)

Mandela, N., *No Easy Walk to Freedom* (Heinemann, 1965)

Sikakane, Joyce, *A Window on Soweto* (IDAF, 1977)

A short geographical background which covers Africa as a whole is:

Fordham, P., *The Geography of African Affairs* (Penguin, 3rd. Edition, 1972)

The following are a small selection of good films on apartheid:

The Heart of Apartheid, BBC, 1968 Black and white.

The Dumping Grounds, Concord and Film Forum, Black and white, made in 1970 for Granada TV. Uses *The Discarded People* by Cosmas Desmond as a basis for looking at life in two Bantu Homelands.

There is no Crisis, Film Forum. Colour, made for Thames TV in 1977 on the Soweto Riots in 1976.

Tale of Two Cities, Film Forum. Johannesburg and Soweto in 1975: a contrast. Colour.

INDEX

NOTE FROM THE AUTHOR

I should like to thank the Extramural Division at the School of Oriental and African Studies for the opportunities recently provided for the study of the History of South Africa. In particular thanks are due to Dr Shula Marks, Reader in African History at the School, for kindly reading and commenting on the typescript of the book and offering suggestions for revision. I should add, of course, that the views expressed and any errors which the book may contain are entirely my own responsibility.

To my wife and family who were very tolerant during the period when the book was being written I offer apologies and thanks. I owe special thanks to my younger daughter who struggled with the typing of a difficult manuscript.

John Addison,
March 1980